The New Theology and Morality

THE NEW
THEOLOGY
AND MORALITY

by
Henlee H. Barnette

THE WESTMINSTER PRESS
Philadelphia

Library of Congress Catalog Card No. 67–11671

Published by The Westminster Press ®
Philadelphia, Pennsylvania

PRINTED IN THE UNITED STATES OF AMERICA

CONTENTS

Preface   7

I. The New Theology: "God Is Dead"   9

   A. *The "Death of God" Quartet*   10
      1. Gabriel Vahanian   10
      2. Paul van Buren   11
      3. William Hamilton   12
      4. Thomas J. J. Altizer   13
   B. *Themes of the New Theology*   14
      1. The "Death of God"   14
      2. Christology   16
      3. Secularity and Secularism   19
      4. Optimism   19
   C. *Critique*   19
      1. *Pro* the New Theology   20
      2. *Contra* the New Theology   23
   D. *"In Defense of God"*   28

II. The New Ethics: "Love Alone"   31

   A. *A Trio of Situationists*   32
      1. Rudolf Bultmann: "As thyself"   32
      2. John A. T. Robinson: "Nothing Prescribed Except
         Love"   35
      3. Joseph Fletcher: "Love and Nothing Else"   38
   B. *Critical Evaluation*   42
      1. Strengths of the Situationists   42
      2. Shortcomings of the Situationists   43
   C. *Toward a More Realistic Morality*   47

III. The New Sex Code: "Permissiveness with Affection"   50

   A. *Sex Attitudes and Standards in American Society*   50
   B. *Causative Factors in Changing Sex Codes*   51
   C. *The* Playboy *Philosophy*   53
   D. *Fruits of the New Freedom*   59
   E. *Some Christian Approaches to Sex*   60
      1. Advocates of the New Sexual Morality   60
      2. Answers to the New Morality   62

F. *Toward a Theology of Sexuality*   65
  1. Key Concepts in the Biblical View of Sex   65
  2. The Case for Chastity   67
  3. The Role of the Church in Sex Education   69

IV. **The New Church: "Servant in a Secular Society"**   72

A. *Secularization of Society*   72
  1. Some Definitions of Secularism and Secularization   73
  2. The Dynamics of Secularization   75
  3. The Degree of Secularization   77

B. *The Servant Church*   79
  1. The New Christology   79
  2. The Servanthood of the Church   80

C. *Critical Evaluation and the Continuing Search*   85
  1. Sensitivity to the Contribution of Secularism   85
  2. Dangerous Trends in Secular Theology   86
  3. Calling and Secular Culture   90

V. **The New Dimensions of War: "Thinking About the Unthinkable"**   91

A. *Wars Past*   91

B. *The New Dimensions of War*   93

C. *Christian Attitudes Toward War*   95
  1. The Pacifist Position   95
  2. The Just War   99
  3. The Holy Crusade   104

D. *Toward a Viable Stance*   105

Notes   109

PREFACE

EXCITING new developments are emerging in contemporary Protestant thought. There is the concept of theology without God as expressed by the "death of God" theologians. Ethics without rules, or "love alone" morality, is now the "growing edge" of Christian ethical thought. The sexual revolution has evoked from some *avant-garde* theologians the so-called "new morality" which lays emphasis upon persons rather than principles in dealing with premarital and extramarital sexual relations. Again, there is the effort to develop new forms of the church with special emphasis upon servanthood in a secular society. And the theologian, the historian, and the scientist are reevaluating traditional views of war in a nuclear age.

Interest in these theological and ethical developments is reflected by the pastor, the denominational leader, and the layman as well as by the theological professor. A chaplain in Vietnam wrote: "Please send me any material you have on the 'death of God' movement. Out here in the jungle some of my men have begun to wonder if God is really dead." Pastors are concerned about an adequate moral authority and wonder if the "new ethic" has any contribution to make toward the clarification of this issue. Many parents are concerned about the growing acceptance among young people of premarital sexual experimentation. Laymen in general are sometimes shocked and confused when they read in popular magazines and the newspapers about the above developments.

It is the aim of this small volume to analyze and to evaluate critically these trends in the hope that the nontheological specialist may better understand them. With only a few changes, the contents of this book were given as lectures to a group of pastors and religious leaders attending the Continuing Theological Education Conference at the Southern Baptist Theological Seminary, Louisville, Kentucky, in December, 1965.

I am solely responsible for the views expressed in this volume. However, I am indebted to others in the preparation of the manuscript for publication. For the invitation to present the lectures at the Continuing Theological Education Conference, I wish to express my appreciation to Dean Penrose St. Amant. To Page Lee, professor of religion, Mars Hill College, and graduate fellow at Southern Seminary, I owe a great debt of gratitude for critically reading the manuscript and offering invaluable suggestions as to structure and style. To Mrs. John Clayton and Henri Etta Bleier who typed the first draft and to Mrs. Glenn Hinson who did the final one, I acknowledge my gratefulness for their proficiency and patience. And finally, to my wife, Helen, a true "helpmeet," for her constructive criticisms and constant encouragement, I am indebted most of all.

H.H.B.

I. THE NEW THEOLOGY:
"GOD IS DEAD"

RECENTLY, both theological journals and the popular press have carried numerous articles describing and debating the ominous-sounding "death of God" theology. As a central motif of a small group of contemporary theologians, the phrase "death of God" symbolizes a new thrust in theological thought. Generally, this radical new theology states that God is dead and that Jesus of Nazareth—the "man for others"—remains, calling men to acts of love to neighbor and the correction of injustices in a secular society.

Among the members of the "death of God club" is a small group of *avant-garde* theologians who hold varying views as to the meaning of God's demise. Indeed, some appear unwilling to take the "death of God" doctrine straight. Hence, they may be classified all the way from the left to the right, from the soft to the hard-core radical on the theological spectrum. The soft radicals still hold to a doctrine of God, but are concerned with how to talk about him in a secular world. Some of them feel that they should not engage in "God talk." They want to declare a moratorium on such speech which may confuse modern man.

For the hard-core radicals the word "God" and the Biblical message in general are problematic. These persons are not concerned with a domesticated God of culture, idols, or theism, or with "the God above God" of Paul Tillich. They are talking about the literal loss of God and any trace of transcendence in the world. They are not talking about the "absence of God" or "the hidden God." They are declaring that God is really dead.

A. THE "DEATH OF GOD" QUARTET

Among the exponents of the "death of God" theology who have delivered their funeral orations are Gabriel Vahanian, William Hamilton, Paul van Buren, and Thomas J. J. Altizer. These radical theologians are youthful—all are under forty-five years of age. They are brilliant and sophisticated, acquainted with classical theology, modern literature such as the novels and plays of Sartre, Greene, Beckett, and Camus, as well as philosophy, particularly the linguistic analysis school. And, finally, they are all largely unsystematic in their approach to theology.

1. Gabriel Vahanian

Born in France in 1927, Vahanian is now professor of religion at Syracuse University. He holds a Baccalauréates-Lettres from Grenoble, and the diploma and Licence en Théologie from the École des Hautes Études of the Sorbonne. From Princeton Theological Seminary he received the master's degree and the doctorate. After teaching at Princeton University for three years, he went to his present post at Syracuse.

Vahanian translated and wrote the introduction to Karl Barth's *The Faith of the Church*. Numerous articles by him have appeared in learned theological journals.[1] His major books are: *The Death of God: The Culture of Our Post-Christian Era,* published by George Braziller, Inc., in New York in 1961; and *Wait Without Idols,* by the same publisher in 1964.

According to Vahanian, we are living in a post-Christian era in which culture is no longer transcendentalist but immanentist, no longer sacral but secular. This stage has been reached because the essentially mythological world view of Christianity has been succeeded by a thoroughgoing scientific view of reality. Hence, God is no longer necessary; he is ir-relevant; he is dead.

Ours is a post-Christian era, contends Vahanian, because: (a) Christianity today is synonymous with religiosity; its appeal to the masses is based on a diluted version of the original faith, making it fashionable to be religious; (b) Christianity no longer inspires and impregnates society; and (c) Christianity no longer dominates culture.[2] Our age may still be religious, but it is post-Christian, a time in which men are merely "gossiping about God." And through a radical im-manentism of "religionitis," Christianity has been reduced to the status of a popular civic religion. In short, Christianity has capitulated to the "Baals of religiosity," a synthesis of nationalism, capitalism, and the American way of life.[3]

Some concepts of God held by those who espouse the re-ligion of the masses are shocking. God is designated as a "Co-Pilot," a "Porter," and a "Cosmic Pal." Such ways of re-ferring to God make one "shudder" because they intimate that God is just "a global hypothesis," an ideal man.[4]

2. Paul van Buren

A second member of the "death of God" quartet is Paul van Buren, who is on the staff of Temple University's department of religion. Prior to his coming to Temple, he was on the faculty of the Episcopal Theological Seminary of the South-west in Austin, Texas, where he was professor of theology. He left this ecclesiastical institution for a position in a secular university (Temple) in order, he maintains, to ask the ques-tion about religion more clearly as it arises in our society than it does in a professional religious context. It was his desire to get outside the "theological circle," which he thinks is becoming increasingly unreal.

Among his articles that can be found in contemporary journals, the most pertinent one for our consideration is "Theology in the Context of Culture."[5] His major book is *The Secular Meaning of the Gospel: Based on an Analysis of Its*

Language, published in 1963 by The Macmillan Company.

Professor van Buren makes use of the tools of linguistic analysis as a method of interpreting the Bible. In so doing, he hopes to find an appropriate way for a Christian to live in a world "come of age" and to confess his faith in Jesus Christ. As a result of this approach, he derives the view that Jesus, the man for others, is the basis of the Christian life. His is a theology without God, a way of life determined by the life of Jesus of Nazareth and the Easter event.

3. William Hamilton

A hard-core radical theologian of the "God is dead" variety is William Hamilton, who teaches systematic theology and ethics at Colgate Rochester Divinity School. A Baptist minister, he was dean of the chapel at Hamilton College before going to Rochester in 1953. Hamilton has written many articles for journals.[6] Among his books, three have special significance for this study: *The Christian Man,* published by The Westminster Press in 1956; *The New Essence of Christianity,* published by Association Press in 1961; and *Radical Theology and the Death of God,* written in collaboration with Thomas J. J. Altizer and published by The Bobbs-Merrill Company, Inc., in 1966.

It is Hamilton's belief that we need to lay claim only to a minimum number of theological doctrines. Hence, he starts afresh with the idea of fragments—those durable items of belief which have survived persecution, creed building, monasticism, and the acids of modern life.[7]

God cannot be objectified, contends Hamilton, for he is not an object among other objects, a person alongside other persons, which would make him a part of this world. This means that we cannot talk about God. We can only talk to him. Hence, we are living in the time of the death of God. For many who call themselves Christians, believing in the time of the "death of God" means that "he is there when we do not want him, in ways we do not want him, and he is not there when we do want him."[8] The cry of dereliction from the cross is sometimes the only Biblical word that can speak to us. "If Jesus can wonder about being forsaken by God," asks Hamilton, "are we to be blamed if we wonder?"[9]

4. Thomas J. J. Altizer

The fourth member of the quartet is Thomas J. J. Altizer, an Episcopal layman and a native of Cambridge, Massachusetts. He received his Ph.D. from the University of Chicago. Since 1956, he has been teaching religion and Bible at Emory University, Atlanta, Georgia. His articles have appeared in several magazines and journals.[10] His books are entitled *Oriental Mysticism and Biblical Eschatology,* published in 1961 by The Westminster Press; *Mircea Eliade and the Dialectic of the Sacred,* by the same press in 1964; *The Gospel of Christian Atheism,* published in 1966 by The Westminster Press; and, in collaboration with William Hamilton, *Radical Theology and the Death of God,* published in 1966 by The Bobbs-Merrill Company, Inc.

A hard-core radical theologian, Altizer maintains that, like ethics and metaphysics, theology has lost its traditional ground and can now be meaningful only when it speaks against its own historical identity. Traditional theology, therefore, must be complemented and challenged by a theology that encounters the new world, even if such a confrontation condemns theology to a negation of itself.[11]

Since God is dead, Altizer thinks that theology can now preserve a Christian form only by speaking of the Incarnate Word that fully confronts time and space. The Christian word moves only by negating its past. Thus neither the Bible nor church history can be accepted as containing more than a provisional or a temporary series of expressions of the Christian word. In this time of the death of God, a new meaning of Christianity has appeared. It not only has a new meaning, but a new reality, created by the kenotic Christ who has finally emptied himself of Spirit, wholly becoming flesh.

B. THEMES OF THE NEW THEOLOGY

Several themes or motifs in the emerging new radical theology must be considered. Not all are equally important to the "death of God" quartet, but each is a fundamental element in the movement.

1. The "Death of God"

Common to all these new theologians is the motif of the death of God. There are varying views on the subject, but all agree that it is the supreme problem in theology. According to Altizer, "the greatest theological problem of our time is an understanding of the meaning of the death of God."[12]

One of the chief sources of the "death of God" theory stems from Friedrich Nietzsche (1844–1900), a German philosopher. Nietzsche says that the gods laughed themselves to death once upon a time, because an old "grim-beard of a god, a jealous one," declared that there is but one God and "Thou shalt have no other gods before me!"[13] The God that remained never had as much life as they. Obedience to him was culture-destroying, and Nietzsche wished to rid the world of such a God in order to liberate the cultural creativity of mankind. This God, made in the image of man, had to die because he was too human and mixed up in human affairs. Says Nietzsche:

> But he—*had to* die: he looked with eyes which beheld *every-thing,*—he beheld men's depths and dregs, all his hidden ignominy and ugliness.
> His pity knew no modesty: he crept into my dirtiest corners. This most prying, over-intrusive, over-pitiful one had to die.
> He ever beheld *me:* on such a witness I would have revenge—or not live myself.
> The God who beheld everything, *and also man:* That God had to die! Man cannot *endure* it that such a witness should live.[14]

According to Nietzsche, God had to die in order that man might be what he is to become—the unlimited creature of culture, the superman.

Dietrich Bonhoeffer, the German theologian who was executed by the Nazis for his role in an effort to assassinate Hitler, also furnishes inspiration for the "death of God" theologians. Van Buren takes as his starting point the following quotation from Bonhoeffer: *"Honesty demands that we recognize that we must live in the world as if there were no God. . . . We stand continually in the presence of the God who makes us live in the world without the God-hypothesis."*[15] Bonhoeffer was describing the need for the church to develop a nonreligious interpretation of Biblical concepts for a secular world "come of age," that no longer finds God necessary as a hypothesis to explain the universe. He certainly believed in God, but not in the "God of the gaps" used to explain the unknowable. The new radical theologians go beyond the hypothesis concept to declare that God is really dead.

The "death of God" theologians also derive support from such modern plays as Samuel Beckett's *Waiting for Godot,* in which God never appears and is therefore pronounced dead, and also Jean-Paul Sartre's *No Exit.* The latter boldly indicates that there is no God, that man must live with courage in a world without him.

Just what is meant by the phrase "death of God"? Does it refer to an event outside of man in some historical or ontological reality? Or does it refer to something within, in that part of the self which does the believing? Or is it a problem of language?

William Hamilton is inclined to avoid the idea of "event" altogether and speak of "death of God" more as "a metaphor describing something that is happening to a particular group of modern Western Christians today."[16] Nevertheless, it is a real loss.

Van Buren avoids the use of the term "God" along with such substitutes as "Ground of Being" and the transcendent. He finds logical difficulty in saying "There is a God," or "God exists," for the term "God" does not lend itself to empirical analysis.[17]

Altizer declares that Christian theology calls upon the Christian theologian to recognize the death of God as a historical event. The Christian must accept the death of God as a final, decisive, and "irrevocable event."[18] Again, the Christian today is called to say "No" to God because God himself has ceased to be present in history. He is present to us only in his absence, and to know the absent or missing God is to know the void that is filled with despair and rebellion. Hence, we must not only celebrate the death of God but will his death.[19]

Vahanian speaks of our living in a time when God is irrelevant, dead.[20] It is an age of radical immanentism, religiosity, and cultural incapacity for God. Vahanian therefore proposes a recovery of Karl Barth's emphasis upon transcendence.

When did the period of *post mortem Dei* begin? Vahanian declares that it occurred when man started to compromise the Biblical conception of God's transcendence and to merge the identity of the Godhead with the identity of man.[21] For van Buren, the death of God came with the rise of technology and modern science which made it necessary to "stick pretty close to what we can experience in ordinary ways."[22]

According to Hamilton, the Christian can celebrate an incarnation in which God actually became flesh and understand this event as effecting the death of God. And though the death of God may not have been historically actualized until the nineteenth century, the event cannot be disassociated from Jesus and his original proclamation.[23] At any rate, the death of God is "a public event in our history."[24] As for Altizer, God negated himself in fully and finally becoming flesh in Jesus. That is, God negated himself in the incarnation and ceased to exist in his original primordial form. In short, God died in Jesus.[25]

2. Christology

Another common motif emerging in the "God is dead" theology is an emphasis upon Christology. But it is a "godless" Christology. However, Hamilton insists that at this time of the death of God we can know enough about Jesus to be his disciples. Obedience to Jesus without Jesus' God is sufficient. Though it is an imperfect obedience, it is nevertheless a choice freely made. Why choose Jesus? Says Hamilton: "Because there is something there, in his words, his life, his way with others, his death, that I do not find elsewhere. I am drawn, and I have given my allegiance. . . . It is a free choice, freely made."[26] And if we are to speak of the divinity of Jesus, we must speak of his weakness and follow him in his humiliation to determine what we mean by God.

Vahanian points out that the new secular Adam becomes the Christic man in the modern novel, another example of radical immanentism in Western culture.[27] Likewise in Protestantism, God's sovereignty has been etiolated, sublimated, and intellectualized.[28] Vahanian appears to have little Christological concern beyond the fact that Christ has been immanentized in man. While he declares that God is dead, he asserts that man is "defined and comprehended by God the Infinite, the Wholly Other."[29]

Paul van Buren attempts to develop a new Christology without theology. Hence Jesus' birth was that of a man who was elected by Yahweh as an expression of his will to fulfill the role of Israel. Says van Buren, Jesus "was the one man who truly existed for others."[30] Christology is the call and response in obedience to the man Jesus. He is "a model of full manhood."[31] Jesus "being for others," by his own choice makes it possible for his disciple to be for others in freedom. This is what happened to the disciples on Easter. Thus van Buren reduces Christian faith to its historical and ethical dimensions.

Altizer also speaks of a Christology without God. Christians are called upon to be "loyal only to Christ, only to the Incarnate Word who has appeared in our flesh, and therefore we should already have been prepared for the appearance of Christ without God."[32] How did it come about that we know that Jesus appears only as an eternal and cosmic Word? The Christological passage in Phil. 2:1–11 furnishes the answer.

As Altizer interprets it, in the "self-emptying" of Christ, the eternal Word, into human form, God died, leaving only the cosmic Word. In this process of kenosis, the primordial God negates himself and Jesus abolishes or reverses religion, annulling the quest for the primordial Beginning.[33] God, therefore, is left behind and "emptied," by the process of "the Incarnation and now the Word *is* only as it is immediately perceived in the act of 'self-perceiving himself.' "[34]

The problem arises as to just where the concrete identity of the Incarnate Word is to be found by the Christian. According to Altizer, the Word is not limited to Jesus of Nazareth, nor is it to be identified with the Christ who is present in the cultus of the church. Rather, the fully Incarnate Word, the end product of kenosis, is present in what William Blake, the artist and poet, called "Experience," that is, the Jesus who is "actually and fully incarnate in every human hand and face."[35] In other words, Jesus is the "Universal Humanity." He is the "Christian name of the totality of Experience, a new actuality created by the abolition of the primordial Being, whose death inaugurates a new humanity liberated from all transcendent norms and meaning."[36] As God who *is* Jesus becomes progressively incarnate in the body of humanity, he loses all of his former visage, until he appears "wherever there is energy and life."[37]

Altizer reasons that Christ is present in humanity and history. We cannot meet our time by remaining bound to a God who is dead. It is only by "freely willing the death of God that we can be open to our time and thereby open to the Christ who is always present, the Word that has actually become united with our flesh."[38] Now the Christian can only "speak the word that is present in our flesh."[39] God, who negated himself, has become the body of a "new humanity" in Jesus which sets us free to give ourselves to the present. The result is "Christocentric atheism."

3. Secularity and Secularism

The new radical theologians stress the fact that we are living in a time of a secularized society and that Christianity calls for secularity. But it does not call for the secularism in which it has often resulted. Bonhoeffer's phrase of "world come of age," in which man no longer believes in any transcendence, is used by them to describe our situation. Hence, the need for what Bonhoeffer called a "nonreligious interpretation of biblical concepts." In other words, they contend that we must have "a secular understanding of the gospel."[40]

For the secular mind, traditional theology has no meaning. Indeed, like ethics and metaphysics, theology has lost its transcendent ground and can be meaningful only as it negates itself and speaks in secular terms. Thus there is an emptiness in "religious language" for the secular mind. "God-talk" has no relevance to the "man come of age" in the technopolis. Therefore, there must be a radical reconstruction in theology. At the hands of the radical theologians, as we have seen, it takes the shape of the death of God and obedience to Jesus, the man for others in love and social concern.

4. Optimism

A final motif emerging in the new radical theology is optimism. It is an optimistic theology. But this does not mean the perfectibility of man and inevitable progress of the old social gospel. Rather, it is a theology "relating itself to a new feeling of hope and optimism in American life today, a conviction that substantive changes in the lives of men can and will be made."[41] Such optimism is to be found today in demonstrations, the Negro revolution, and other protest movements for social justice.

C. CRITIQUE

Already critics are attacking the new radical theologians in various ways and at several points. Word comes that someone has written on the walls of a New York subway station: God is Dead! (Signed) Nietzsche. Nietzsche is Dead! (Signed) God. From the comic strip angle, there is the picture of two fish in a bowl. One says to the other: "If God is dead, who changes the water every day?"

Serious criticisms of the "God is dead" theologians can be found in several current articles. From these and other sources the following critique is offered. It should be noted that any genuine critique includes both the pros and the cons of the issue.

1. Pro *the New Theology*

The new theological movement, first of all, is forcing us to reexamine seriously the doctrine of God. The late Paul Tillich, whose classical statement that we must seek the "God above God," the God above the man-made God of traditional theism, concedes: "I say yes to this movement insofar as it points to something above the symbolic language concerning God."[42] But he says no to this movement on the ground that its exponents are abandoning all symbolic language about God.

Certainly there is need to bury the God of radical immanentism, the God who has become homogenized with man, the God of our contemporary religiosity. This God must go, for he no longer has meaning for modern man. There is no relevance or healing for the ills of humanity in this God. In the words of Jeremiah: "In vain you have used many medicines; there is no healing for you." The "God of the gaps," the *"deus ex machina"* whom we are attempting to save from death by artificial respiration, has no healing powers and therefore should be discarded. In Julian Huxley's words, this God should be rejected as the "last fading smile of a cosmic Cheshire Cat."[43]

It is imperative that we return now to the God of revelation, the God of Abraham, Isaac, and Jacob. This is the God who is supremely revealed in the face of Jesus Christ, and who is "the same yesterday and today and for ever" (Heb. 13:8).

In the second place, these new theologians have made a contribution in exposing our "religionitis" or institutional religiosity so prevalent in the churches today. Vahanian with his new iconoclasm has leveled devastating strictures at the reduction of the Christian faith to a "civic religion" in America. He traces the whole process of the movement from the original theocentrism of the Bible to the conception of God as a "Cosmic Pal," which is but another step toward universal anthropomorphism in a secular world.

Another value of the new theology is that it calls attention to the necessity of theological renewal. All of the theologians in this movement are characterized by an openness, a sincere desire to reconstruct theology so as to make it more meaningful and relevant to "man come of age." Theology, if it is genuine theology, is dynamic, not static, and seeks to speak to men in the historical, concrete situation where moral decision and action must take place.

Theological creeds and propositions tend to become dated, stereotyped, ossified, and therefore must be updated. Christian creeds and statements of faith should be revised at least every fifty years to make them meaningful for a new generation and a changed social milieu.

A stress on the significance of ethics is another strong factor among the *avant-garde* theologians. William Hamilton places more emphasis on ethical thought and action than do the other three men being considered. He calls attention to the radical nature of Jesus' ethics. To confront Jesus is to confront the radical demand of his life and his teaching.[44] Obedience to Christ in faith issues in a "style of life" characterized by a tentative imitation of him. He describes choices open along a broad spectrum ranging from rebellion, activism, transforming the world, a break with conformist culture to resignation, receiving and suffering in the world, and the search for a concealed break within culture. Such a style of life, he admits, may do for today, though not for tomorrow.[45]

Elsewhere Hamilton deals with social ethics. Christ is "a

place to be" and the place of Christ is in the midst of the Negro's struggle for equality, in the new forms of technological society, in the city, with the needy neighbor and the enemy.[46] He goes on to say that in the time of the death of God, "we have a place to be," and this is "not before an altar; it is in the world."[47] Hamilton declares that this is what the form of love looks like. "It is a love," he says, "that takes place in the middle of the real world, the ugly, banal, godless, religious world of America today."[48]

Altizer briefly discusses the ethical message of Jesus along with myth and ethics in Buddhism and Christianity.[49] Here he finds the ethics of Jesus to be radical, so radical as to leave "no room for a positive attitude toward civic, political and cultural responsibilities."[50] The ethics of Jesus and his Kingdom were predominantly eschatological, resting upon world negation. Repentance and faith were requisites to entrance into the Kingdom. But in the history of the church, the eschatological factor was transformed into a this-worldly religion. The dialectical tension between the Kingdom of God and this world was lost.

For van Buren, Christianity is an agapeistic way of life. He is concerned with what religion can do for man today. The man, Jesus of Nazareth, the historical man, is our "model of full manhood."[51] "The demand for obedience, humility, bearing one another's burdens, love, and service is based on an appeal to these characteristics in Jesus himself."[52] He agrees with Bonhoeffer that "the experience of transcendence is Jesus' being-for-others. His omnipotence, omniscience, and omnipresence arise solely out of his freedom from self, out of his freedom to be for others even unto death."[53] Hence, the Christian is to be obedient to Christ in freedom and imitate him in being free from self and wholly for others. Thus van Buren builds an ethical faith around the man, Jesus of Nazareth.

The new theologians use practical means of promoting their theories. In 1965 two meetings were held, one at Drew University in Madison, New Jersey, and one at Emory University in

Atlanta, Georgia, for the reading of papers and discussions about "God is dead" theology. Also, there is talk of producing a journal for a growing and eager readership.

2. Contra *the New Theology*

Numerous strictures are directed at the thought of the new theologians.[54] The following criticisms appear to be pertinent and valid.

First, there is an ambiguity in the talk of the "God is dead" cult. Actually, there is a reserve in most of these theologians to come right out and say that God is dead, period. Due to their murky dialectics, it is difficult to know whether God is dead, is in eclipse, or is just "edged out of our world." After telling us, in one hundred and fifty-nine pages of his book *The New Essence of Christianity,* that God has disappeared, Hamilton asserts that the new style of life he has been describing may do for today and that it is in this day that we are to obey God! There seems to be a reluctance to at least bury the corpse of God. He may appear when we don't want him and be away when we do want him. At times Hamilton talks about the absence of God. But then again he speaks of his presence.[55]

Altizer is consistent in his statements that God is dead. For him, God is not simply "hidden" or in "eclipse"; he is literally dead. Furthermore, the historical Jesus himself is dead, which is a particular expression of the deeper reality of the death of God. In short, Altizer holds to the historicity of the death of God and of Jesus. Perhaps he is speaking metaphorically, but he gives no indication that he is.

In the light of this fact, one wonders what Altizer means by the "word of faith" which he claims cannot be identified with an eternal God or understood as a particular expression of an unchanging deity. All that is left is the Incarnate Word in the flesh. How can he talk about the Incarnate Word without God? For in the beginning was the Word and the Word was God who became flesh (John 1:1, 14). Altizer's Incarnate Word appears to be "a wordless Word, an incarnation without flesh."[56]

It is difficult to ascertain whether both Vahanian and van Buren really believe that God is dead, that he has become man, or just "edged out of our world." All that remains for van Buren is Jesus with a semblance of the historic faith in him by the empirical method. For Altizer, nothing remains but a vague notion of the Incarnate Word.

This brings us to the problem of Christology. For Hamilton, Jesus is the man for others in his humility and suffering, the paradigm of the ethical life in human relations. Van Buren sees Jesus the man as the bearer of freedom, a call and response Christology. Altizer conceives of Christ as the Incarnate Word with the loss of his humanity. But he thinks that we can speak of the Word when we say yes to the moment before us. His concept of the incarnation is a gross distortion of kenotic Christology taught by the apostle Paul.

In Phil. 2:1–11, Paul is concerned with the ethical problem of humility in the primitive church at Philippi and he uses Christ as the example to follow. Now since Altizer's view of the incarnation stands or falls on the correct interpretation of a part of this passage in Philippians, it is quoted as follows:

> Do nothing from selfishness or conceit, but in humility count others better than yourselves. Let each of you look not only to his own interests, but also to the interests of others. Have this mind among yourselves, which you have in Christ Jesus, who, though he was in the form of God, did not count equality with God a thing to be grasped, but emptied himself, taking the form of a servant, being born in the likeness of men. And being found in human form he humbled himself and became obedient unto death, even death on a cross. Therefore God has highly exalted him and bestowed on him the name which is above every name, that at the name of Jesus every knee should bow, in heaven and on earth and under the earth, and every tongue confess that Jesus Christ is Lord, to the glory of God the Father.

The word "form" (*morphē*) from Homer to the New Testament means a form as it appears to a person. It means outward form and has nothing to do with nature or attributes. Paul is not interested in what Jesus gave up and what attributes of God he retained, but in the humility of Jesus. Paul goes on to say that Jesus "emptied" himself (accusative); that is, he did not empty something from himself, but emptied himself from one form and to another form. The form is different but the substance is the same. He took on the "likeness" of men. "Likeness" asserts similarity, but denies identity, for he is more than man. He took the "form," outward appearance, of a man, even a slave, and went to his death on the cross. With this example of Christ's humility as the Christian's example, it should not be so difficult to put others above oneself.

In the above passage, there is not the slightest hint that God died on the cross, that all that was God merged into humanity through Jesus, and that the cosmic Word is to be encountered in every "face and hand." Christ was made in the "likeness" of man, not identical with him.

After pondering the Jesus of Hamilton, van Buren, and Altizer, Robert Nelson asks: "Will the real Jesus please step forward?" But the three stay where they are. For to tell the truth, none is the real Jesus of Biblical revelation![57]

These men appear to substitute "Jesus-language" for "God-language." But if the God of Jesus is dead, then Jesus is merely a good man. If the reality of God is revealed in Christ as the Bible teaches, then Jesus must be in some fashion God himself. Daniel Day Williams sums up the inner contradictions of these men with an aphorism: "There is no God, and Jesus is his only begotten son."[58] Thus Jesus the Christ of God is reduced to Jesus of Nazareth the man. All that is left is a Jesus-inspired morality of involvement in a secular world.

The optimistic bias of the *avant-garde* theologians is also open to criticism. In contrast to the secular "God is dead" champions—Albert Camus, Jean-Paul Sartre, Kafka, Heidegger, and Beckett, who hold that the death of God makes this world a night of hell—the hard-core radicals see a new hope and optimism, especially in American life. Just how radical is a theology that changes when the national mood changes?

The optimism of Hamilton and his colleagues presents three tendencies characteristic of the liberal social gospelers. First, they tend to identify Christianity and the Kingdom of God entirely with social action and progress. But the Kingdom of God is more than social involvement and is not wholly realizable in secular history. Secondly, these men almost completely overlook the demonic forces in culture and in man himself. Thirdly, their optimism about the possibilities of love is questionable. Love tends to break down in the "collective brutalities" of society.

"If God-language," as Langdon Gilkey notes, "is meaningless to today's suburbanite, then surely love-language [at least when it has to do with giving oneself selflessly for one's neighbor!] is to him ridiculous."[59]

Moreover, there is a real question as to whether modern secular man has "come of age." Is he not the same man he was centuries ago with his sins of selfishness, greed, pride, self-sufficient finitude, and his need of God?

Again, none of the quartet has much appreciation for the church as an institution. They are influenced by Kierkegaard in developing the idea that organized Christianity is a kind of idolatry, obscuring the real message of the gospel behind a smoke screen of outmoded and irrelevant cultural forms.

Hamilton declares that the answer to the banal question about whether the theologian goes to church is "No." He is not interested.[60] Altizer writes that "contemporary theology must be alienated from the Church. . . . The theologian must exist outside the Church; he can neither proclaim the Word, celebrate the sacraments, nor rejoice in the presence of the Holy Spirit. Before contemporary theology can become itself, it must first exist in silence."[61]

According to Hamilton, the church must be defined as present "wherever Christ is being formed among men in the world. . . . It now has no outlines, no preaching, sacraments, or liturgy."[62] He agrees with Bonhoeffer that our Christianity today will be confined "to praying for and doing right by our fellow men. Christian thinking, speaking and organization must be reborn out of this praying and this action."[63]

As for the mission of the church, van Buren holds that it is the way of love, the way toward the neighbor, not the way of trying to make others into Christians. The Christian's mission "is simply to be a man, as this is defined by Jesus of Nazareth."[64] In short, the church has talked too much to the world for the Christian to evangelize. Theology is for the church, he declares, and should take place in the church. Then he appears to contradict all of this by declaring that theology is responsible to human society, not to the church. Traditionally, theology has been a discipline in service of the church, but now van Buren asserts that its orientation is humanistic, not divine. Rather, its "norms must lie in the role it performs in human life."[65]

This view tends to deprive the Christian faith of any mystical elements. Such efforts to make Christianity palatable to the intelligentsia negates the mystery of God in Christ, his incarnation, death, resurrection, and the contemporaneity of the Holy Spirit. Rudolf Otto, in *The Idea of the Holy*, notes that there is an element of irrationality in religion that cannot be intellectualized. If Jesus is not divine and only a man for others, then what is the ultimate significance of following him? Why not Socrates or Bonhoeffer? Both died for their convictions.

Finally, the new theologians have little to say about the third Person of the Trinity. Presumably he died with the first Person, leaving only the human Jesus (in the case of Hamilton and van Buren) and the Incarnate Word (Altizer). Neglect of the role of the Holy Spirit in conversion, as the enabler of the Christian life and as guide in moral decisions, is one of the fundamental weaknesses of the whole "God is dead" movement. To follow Jesus and to pattern one's life after his example is simply impossible without the energizing power of the Holy Spirit.

After reading the basic works and numerous articles by the

radical theologians, one gets the feeling that they, in all honesty, should not go on using the Bible, teaching and talking about Christianity in the classrooms, wearing religious wraps over their unbelief, but should join the unhypocritical humanists. But, on second thought, these men are describing rather accurately our present situation in which traditional ways of talking about God are no longer grasped by modern man in a meaningful fashion.

One wonders also why Hamilton, van Buren, and Altizer keep calling themselves theologians. Theology has to do with God. Hence, the "death of God" concept appears to contradict the very rationality of those who hold to such a faith. Yet, they are discussing God, though for them he has disappeared or died.

D. "IN DEFENSE OF GOD"

God is not without his defenders among numerous theologians and evangelists. Dr. John Bennett, president of Union Theological Seminary in New York City, takes issue with those who say that "God is dead."[66] He concedes that there are no scientific proofs of God, but claims that there are "intimations" of his existence. These "pointers" to God will not of themselves convince the atheists but may prepare the way for the vision of God in revelation.

Bennett's major intimations for God are that the world of experience makes sense only by faith in God; that man has a sense of absolute obligation and a willingness to die rather than falsely to affirm the powers of the world; that man has the impulse to worship and to give himself in devotion and sacrifice to something beyond himself; and that the actual experience of the healing of grace in the midst of common experience is a hint of something which transcends our closed systems of thought.

Evangelist Billy Graham, in an interview with the editors of *U.S. News & World Report*, declared emphatically that God is not dead.[67] His arguments for belief in God are: (1) All people have religion and believe in some sort of God; (2) one has to breathe and there is air; to drink water and there is water; likewise, one has a hunger for God and there is a God; (3) if there is no God, then lying, murder—anything you want to do—is permitted; and (4) the Bible says there is a God as revealed in Jesus Christ.

For this writer, one of the strongest evidences of God is that of a sense of his presence in human experience and in the world. The transformation in personality that issues from faith and commitment to God in Christ is undeniable. Witness the change in the lives of millions of God's children through the centuries of Christianity.

Obviously the experience of God's working in the individual and the world cannot be established through ordinary sensory data. Nor does it lend itself to empirical scientific verification. But it must be remembered that all experience is not sensory, for one can have experience other than that of touch, taste, smell, and sound. There are the realities of loyalty, love, and honesty, between subjects and objects, that are just as real as sensory experience. As John Baillie observes, these subtle senses beyond bodily senses enable us to *perceive* something otherwise not perceptible, to perceive it and not merely to *conceive* it. A case in point is the sense of the presence of God.[68] The reductive naturalist, therefore, who claims that the only knowledge of reality is through sensory experience by scientific verification cannot even verify *this* proposition by scientific verification.

Man's very being longs for the living God (Ps. 42). Augustine put it well: "Thou hast formed us for Thyself, and our hearts are restless till they find rest in Thee."[69] The God who answers to man's thirst for him is no more dead today than he was when Nietzsche and others in the last century declared so eloquently this doctrine. The problem of modern man is that he is so busy running from reality that he is unaware of the presence of God. Fleeing from the wrath of his brother Esau whom he had cheated out of his birthright, Jacob spent the night at a place that he called Bethel. There God spoke to him in a dream. When Jacob awoke from his sleep, he declared: "Surely the Lord is in this place; and I did not know it" (Gen. 28:16).

Some people have lost a sense of the presence of God in the "everydayishness" of modern existence. Dr. John R. Claypool has vividly illustrated this fact from the following incident:

> In the back of our chapel here at Crescent Hill there is a stained glass window depicting Christ standing at a door knocking. A mother told me once that her little child kept looking at it and asked one night: "Why don't the people in the house ever let Jesus in?" The mother was taken by surprise and said nothing for a moment, and so the child began to answer her own question. "Maybe they're out driving some place and aren't at home, or maybe they've got the television on so loud they can't hear, or maybe they're living in the back of the house and don't realize He is knocking."[70]

God is not dead, but on every man's doorstep. "Behold, I stand at the door and knock; if any one hears my voice and opens the door, I will come in to him and eat with him, and he with me." (Rev. 3:20.)

II. THE NEW ETHICS:
"LOVE ALONE"

OURS is an age of moral crisis and confusion. Adrift upon a sea of conflicting moral dilemmas, modern man himself has become the "measure of all things," including his moral behavior. He has no certain measuring rod for gauging character and conduct, no supreme moral authority for his life in a complex society. His predicament is that of the people described by the prophet Isaiah "who call evil good and good evil, who put darkness for light and light for darkness, who put bitter for sweet and sweet for bitter!" (Isa. 5:20). Another Biblical statement from the dark ages of the Judges describes our current moral anarchy: "In those days there was no king in Israel; every man did what was right in his own eyes" (Judg. 21:25).

Some theologians are keenly aware of the malaise in current Protestant moral thought. Professor Sidney Cave concludes: "Outside the Roman Church, there is now no consensus of opinion in regard either to the method or content of Christian Ethics."[1] But both Catholic and Protestant ethics appear to be equally impotent for today. Neither has been able to provide man with adequate ethical insight and guidance in a technological age.

As traditionally interpreted, Christian ethics appear to be inadequate as a moral guide in our complex culture. Indeed, as the editor of *Look* magazine declares: "We are witnessing the death of the old morality. In our world of masses of people,

jet-age travel, nuclear power and fragmented families, condi-
tions are changing so fast that the etablished moral guidelines
have been yanked from our hands."[2]

This, in spite of the fact that our century has had great
theological ethicists in the Niebuhrs, Tillich, Barth, and Brunner. The ethical thrusts of these men appear to be waning, and
the search is on for a new approach to ethics. Not only theologians but scientists are calling for a new morality. Harlow
Shapley, the Harvard astronomer, declares: "We need an
ethical system suitable for now—for this atomic age—rather
than for the human society of two thousand years ago."[3]

A. A TRIO OF SITUATIONISTS

In response to the challenge of the moral situation, a group
of theologians is emerging who espouse what has come to be
known as the "new morality," "contextual ethics," or "Situa-
tionsethik." This new thrust in Christian ethics stresses the
primacy of love without law. It is a reaction against the old
morality of laws, rules, and moral principles as guides to
conduct.

This approach to moral issues is inductive rather than deductive, beginning with concrete facts of a specific ethical
situation rather than with moral laws or principles. It insists
that the demand of God must be perceived in the moment of
concrete experience rather than in principles or laws of conduct abstracted from the moment.

1. Rudolf Bultmann: "As thyself"

"Radical obedience" in love is the central motif in the ethics
of Rudolf Bultmann. By this he means *to listen for and re-
spond to the Word of God speaking through the situation in
which one exists.*"[4] Radical obedience is an eschatological
ethic. God's reign is breaking in now, and impinging now, sum-
moning men to live now in terms of God's coming reign. This
eschatological content demands radical obedience in the present tense.

Thus in his idea of radical obedience, Bultmann is attempting to synthesize the older liberal view of the ethical teaching of Jesus to be applied to problems and the thoroughgoing eschatologists (Weiss and Schweitzer) who held that the ethical imperatives of Jesus were "interim ethics." Bultmann holds that the eschatological and ethical teachings of Jesus cannot be separated.[5] Hence, decision and obedience have their ground in the eschatological teachings of Jesus. For the future forces impinge upon man in the *present,* requiring of him decision for God or the world now. Readiness for God's future demands obedience to his will in the present. The content of radical obedience is love, and no one is ready for God's reign unless he loves his neighbor whom he meets. Man is to live and love his neighbor as if the end, the *eschaton,* were present. Here, "end" does not mean chronological end, but the end of a false understanding of ourselves and history. It is the end time of ultimate judgment and decision.

Bultmann makes a distinction between "formal" obedience and "radical" obedience. Judaic legalism, in which the law had lost its content but retained its form, is characteristic of the former. Formal obedience, therefore, has to do with conformity to external rules. Radical obedience involves the total person, his being and his doing. Man is obedient in his being as well as in his doing.

God's demand, according to Bultmann, is not an abstract system of ethics apart from the demand of the moment, but to be radically obedient in the moment. Man "hears" God's word in the concrete situation. Somehow the demand of the moment is discernible, for God's demand is written into the situation. If we do not hear it, the fault is ours. The self cannot bring with it any standards of the past, for it is a standardless moment, but allows the moment to create its own unique demand. Hence, the moment contains *all* that is necessary to understand the will of God.[6]

However, Bultmann does admit that what the moment demands is made clearer by a knowledge of precedents and consequents. But a moral decision made in relation to one's neighbor in the moment is never determined by such knowledge. Man knows what he ought to do in the moment, but not out of rational analysis or previous ethical knowledge. The morally good action cannot be known until it is revealed in the situation. It is disclosed out of the situation of the moment.

But what does the moment demand? It does *not* demand a *what* (a specific action) but a *that* (that one is to be responsible). It demands that we love in every situation. The *what* or the content of love must be left to the individual in his concrete situation. God does not specifically tell us *what* we are to do, but *that* we are responsible, allowing us to choose how we are to be specifically responsible. For example, the great commandment of love says nothing about the content of love, only that we are to love our neighbor as ourselves. Says Bultmann, "The demand for love needs no formulated stipulations," as seen in the parable of the good Samaritan.[7]

Bultmann argues that everyone *knows* how to love his neighbor because he knows how he wishes to be loved. The love commandment simply tells us we ought to love our neighbor, not what we must do to love him. "As thyself" is the key to the content of the demand of God in the moment. One simply has not heard the call of the neighbor if he legalistically asks the question what he is to do.[8]

For Bultmann, love is not emotion or sympathy, for love does not depend on man's feelings, but on the command of God. Man loves because the neighbor is in need, and his need constitutes the demand of God in the moment. Thus the neighbor is every person who meets us in the moment with a concrete need.

By now it is obvious that radical obedience as Bultmann sees it cannot be the ground for a systematic theory of ethics because it refers to a specific and concrete relation to existence. Once radical obedience is conceptualized, it loses its concreteness, historicity, and existentiality which distinguishes it from other ethics.

As we have seen, Bultmannian radical obedience operates out of an eschatological view of history. It also involves an existential view of man. At this point, Bultmann was greatly influenced by the philosopher Martin Heidegger; namely, his presupposition that *man's being is a possibility of being*. Human existence is not a static being with a "fixed" nature, but a being constantly choosing itself. Man is always in the midst of *choosing who he is*. Therefore, human *nature* possesses no constants that may be relied upon in any given situation. Hence, there can be no systematic ethics organized only on the basis of human nature. Man is always striving toward a goal, but the goal is left undetermined by his ontological structure. Death to the old life and *becoming* is the law of the obedient life. Man's possibility for the authentic life can only be achieved in response to the proclamation of the gospel. This is what he calls *ontic* possibility for authenticity.[9]

Man lives in his *intentionality*. He is in search for authentic selfhood. Man knows that he *is* not what he *ought* to be. He knows that his life consists in a struggle to become an authentic self, that is, to really be himself, to be what he *ought* to be. The theologian sees the demand of God as none other than authentic selfhood. In response to the deed of God in Christ, man becomes a new being, an authentic self.[10]

2. John A. T. Robinson: "Nothing Prescribed Except Love"

Another contextualist in ethics is John A. T. Robinson, Bishop of Woolwich. In 1963, Robinson published a small volume entitled *Honest to God*,[11] which had a bombshell effect on both sides of the Atlantic. The response ranged from high praise to severe condemnation. The debate about the book continues unabated.[12] Robinson borrows from Bonhoeffer's idea of a "religionless Christianity," and Jesus the "man for others"; from Bultmann's demythologizing theory; and from Tillich's concept of God as the "Ground of all Being." Theism is gone, Robinson says, because men today do not find God "up there" or "out there." As the "Ground of Being," however, he may still be found in the depth of experience. Thus Robinson abandons the idea of spatial transcendence, concluding that God is the "Ground of all Being." Christologically Robinson follows the New English Bible: "What God was, the Word was." In other words, if one looked at Jesus, one saw God: "He who has seen me has seen the Father" (John 14:9). Drawing on Bonhoeffer, Robinson says "Jesus is 'the man for others', the one in whom Love has completely taken over, the one who is utterly open to, and united with, the Ground of his being."[13] To be in Christ is to be a new being. "It is the life of 'the man for others', the love whereby we are brought completely into one with the Ground of our being, manifesting itself in the unreconciled relationships of our existence."[14]

Robinson's chapter on ethics is labeled "The New Morality," a popular cognate of "situation ethics." It appears that this phrase was inspired by Pope Pius XII in 1952 to describe situational ethics in a radio message, "The Christian Conscience." Here he made the terms "existential" and "situational" synonymous. Four years later "situational ethics" was labeled "the new morality" by the Supreme Sacred Congregation of the Holy Office and banned from all academies and seminaries.[15] For Robinson, morality is situational; that is, response to the specific, immediate grasp of the will of God rather than dependence on rules or natural law. "Man come of age" demands a "new morality" and Robinson proceeds to provide it.

A rather sharp contrast is drawn between the "old" and the "new" morality. The old is deductive, beginning with absolute standards, eternally valid, remaining unchanged, and to be applied in the midst of change. The new morality is inductive and begins from "the other end," namely, "unselfregarding *agape*" in the particular situation. *Agapē* is the one constant element in the distinctively Christian response in every age, for it produces in the Christian, however diversely placed, a style of life that is recognizably the same.[16]

The old morality starts with principles, the new with persons. It proceeds empirically from the particular to the general.

Traditional deductive morality tends to be *antihumanist,* being oriented to supernatural principles which sometimes take precedence over persons and to which they must conform regardless of the circumstances. The new morality emphasizes "the priority of persons over principles."[17]

Robinson admits, however, that society needs certain laws and rules to survive. Actions such as stealing, lying, killing, and committing adultery are wrong because they are destructive to human relations. But he says that we cannot mean that these are always wrong, as, for example, killing in a just war may be right.[18]

Also there are blocks of ethical teachings in the Gospels and epistles for the ordering of the life of the church, and these come to us through the church. But these teachings for the early church can be a distortion in the church today. The ultimate criterion of conduct is not an ethical code, but selfless and sacrificial *agapē* in the moment of decision. The one important thing that really counts is "treating persons as persons with unconditional seriousness."[19] This is the end at which the new morality begins.

According to Robinson, the *content* of Christian morals changes with changing situations. A change, for example, in biological, technological, or psychological knowledge may modify our understanding of the responsibility involved. He then proceeds to supply several illustrations. Take the problem of divorce. The traditional teaching of the church is that marriage ought never to be dissolved. In the case of Protestants, of course, divorce may be allowed for adultery. Divorce, therefore, is always wrong with the one exception of fornication. The Matthean exception is an addition by the writer (Matt. 5:32) and has been made a law by church and state. To say that all divorce involves adultery is not true. If a wife had already committed fornication, one cannot, technically, make her an adulteress, for this she has already made herself. Any divorce of a wife is to make her morally and not legally an adulteress. Jesus also speaks of *lust* as the moral equivalent of adultery, but no one treats it as legislation. Paul, himself, allows persons who become Christians to divorce their pagan partners if these will not live with them (I Cor. 7:12–16). The practice of cohabitation in celibacy (I Cor. 7:36–38) in the teachings of Paul would hardly be acceptable today. Indeed, cohabitation in celibacy would be considered a scandal—certainly among the clergy![20]

All of this is to say that while the church must have rules, these rules are not necessarily timeless. Take the problem of homosexuality, for example. Love also is to determine our attitude toward the homosexual. Pressures from the empirical side have already forced us to alter our attitude toward this problem. In 1957, the Wolfenden Report stated that "homosexual behaviour between consenting adults in private should no longer be a criminal offence."[21] In the case of homosexuality, inductive ethics begins with the empirical, with persons, and through love these are to be helped to solve their problems.

At the heart of Robinson's ethics is love. He sums it up:

> Love alone, because, as it were, it has a built-in moral compass, enabling it to "home" intuitively upon the deepest need of the other, can allow itself to be directed completely by the situation.[22]

Love alone is the only ethic "which offers a point of constancy in a world of flux and yet remains absolutely free for, and free over, the changing situation."[23] Admittedly, we must have laws and conventions in society, for these are "the dykes of love" in a world that has lost its way. But they must be defined situationally and not prescriptively, in terms of persons and not principles. His is a plea for the priority of love over everything else. This is the only ethic for "man come of age."[24]

3. Joseph Fletcher: "Love and Nothing Else"

The third person of the triumvirate that espouses "love alone" ethics is Joseph Fletcher, who is professor of social ethics at the Episcopal Theology School, Cambridge, Massachusetts. He claims that basically there are only three approaches to making moral decisions—legalistic, antinomian, and situational (a way between rules of legalism and antinomian unprincipledness).[25]

For Fletcher, Christian situation ethics has only one norm—the *agapē* of the commandment to love God and neighbor. All rules, principles, ideals, and norms are only *contingent*, only valid if perchance they serve love in any situation. These may serve as *illuminators*, but not *directors*, in moral decisions. Hence, "*only* love and reason really count when the chips are down!"[26] In capsule form, situational strategy is a method that proceeds from one law, *agapē* (love), to *sophia* (wisdom) of the church and culture, to *kairos* (moment of decision, the fullness of time) in which the responsible self in the situation decides whether *sophia* can serve love there.[27]

Four presuppositions are inherent in this approach to decision-making: pragmatism (a strategy which holds that to be correct or right a thing must *work*, but in situation ethics love is the standard of rightness); relativism (love is the constant and all else variable); positivism (theological positivism in which faith propositions are affirmed voluntaristically and not rationalistically); and personalism (people and not things are at the center of concern). Put together, these principles take the shape of action, existence, and eventfulness. Hence, the situation ethic is one of "*making* decisions rather than 'looking them up' in a manual of prefab rules."[28]

In situation ethics, conscience (moral consciousness) is a function, not a faculty. Conscience is taken into account only when it is acting and deciding. Moreover, situation ethics is concerned with antecedent, not consequent, conscience, "with prospective decision-making rather than with retrospective judgment-passing."[29]

The core of situation ethics consists of six propositions.[30] Proposition one points to the nature of value, the "rock bottom" issue in all ethics—namely, the only intrinsic good is love: "nothing else at all." On the reverse side, the only thing that is intrinsically bad is malice. Love is a predicate with men, and only with God is it a property because God *is* love and finite men only *do* love. No law, principle, or value is good as such—not life, truth, chastity, property, marriage, or anything but love. Hence such acts as lying and suicide are not always wrong, for these are contingent upon the situation.

In his second proposition, Fletcher declares that love is the ultimate norm of Christian decision. Jesus himself set aside the law of the Sabbath for the higher law of love in the healing of the man with the withered hand, and Paul was permissive about circumcision. *Agapē* seeks "the neighbor's good radically, nonpreferentially."[31] Hence, Christian ethics is not "a scheme of codified conduct," but separates "the creed from the *code,* but not from conduct" as some critics charge.[32]

Love is the only norm of conduct. Jesus put his stamp of approval on the translegality of the action of David, who, when he was hungry, went into the house of God and ate the bread of the Presence which was not lawful except for the priests (Matt. 12:3–4). Thus, the ultimate norm of conduct is love and nothing else.

Proposition three equates love and justice, for the latter is love distributed. Love of the generic "neighbor" in the teachings of Jesus and Paul must be converted into the plural "neighbors." Hence, justice is love working out its problems; it is Christian love using its head and calculating its duties.[33] Justice, therefore, is love distributed.

Proposition four embodies the view that love wills the neighbor's good whether we like him or not. Love and liking are not the same thing, for the former is benevolence and good will. There is nothing sentimental about love. It is not an emotional but an attitudinal ethic, volitional, and can be commanded.

Proposition five declares that only the end justifies the means. Classical Christian ethics accepted the doctrine that "the end does not justify the means." Fletcher askes that, if it doesn't, what does? The answer is, "Nothing!"[34] But, unless justified by some end in view, any action is meaningless, pointless. Referring to Paul, who says that it is not being "lawful" that makes a thing good, but whether it is expedient, edifying, constructive, Fletcher makes his case for "agapeic expediency," for only love can make a thing "lawful."[35]

To the question, "Does an evil means always nullify a good end?" Fletcher says, "No," for it all depends upon the situation. In this world of relativities, "we may do what *would* be evil in some contexts if *in this one* love gains the balance."[36] For example, if the emotional and spiritual welfare of both parents and children in a *particular* family can best be served by a divorce, then love requires it.

The sixth proposition of Fletcher attempts to validate every judgment within its own context. Hence, decisions should be made situationally, not prescriptively. He accepts Emil Brunner's principle that the divine command is always the same in the *Why*, but always different in the *What*.[37] Christians should not, therefore, underestimate this relativism in ethics. They must put away their childish rules and learn love's tactics.[38]

Fletcher, in his postscript, notes that situationism in Christian ethics is a reaction against legalism. Contextual or situational ethics, he feels, is freedom from legalism and the sense of guilt it engenders. Man is free "when we tailor our ethical cloth to fit the back of each occasion."[39] This is what he calls "neocasuistry." Like classical casuistry it is case-focused, concrete, and concerned to bring Christian imperatives to bear upon practical issues. However, it is unlike classical casuistry in that it repudiates any attempt to prescribe "real-life decisions in their existential particularity."[40] It is always "a casuistry obedient to love."[41] The tactical formula for the strategy of love is: "*The indicative plus the imperative equals the normative. What is, in the light of what love demands, shows what ought to be.*"[42] He concludes that Christian ethics is not "a scheme of living according to a code but a continuous effort to relate love to a world of relativities through a casuistry obedient to love; its constant task is to work out the strategy and tactics of love, for Christ's sake."[43]

B. CRITICAL EVALUATION

We have briefly examined "love alone" ethics and three persons who champion it. A critical analysis of their conclusions reveals both strengths and weaknesses. These are suggested below.

1. Strengths of the Situationists

One cannot but be impressed with the ethical seriousness of Bultmann, Robinson, and Fletcher. Christianity is an ethical faith as well as a theological one. It is a way of life undergirded by faith in God as revealed in Jesus Christ. It is always refreshing to read theologians who include both theological and ethical dimensions in their presentation of Christianity.

Love is the central motif of Christian ethics for all three men. In this they follow the New Testament pattern. Jesus laid down no rules for Christian conduct. He was not a new Moses handing down laws to govern behavior. Rather, he presented illustrations and principles of the Christian style of life. Christian morality, therefore, cannot be reduced to a legalistic set of rules applicable to every person in all situations.

Concern for persons in preference to abstract moral rules does have merit. Traditional morality with its "Thou shalt not's" is hardly the approach to take when counseling with people who are in serious trouble. To offer such persons a code without compassion does appear to be "antihumanist." The Christian way of meeting the spiritual needs of men is to be redemptive, and this means to treat them as persons. For example, the notion that chastity is a part of charity, the expression of caring enough for a person not to use him or her, is an excellent one. While this has Kantian overtones, it is also in keeping with the Christian ethic of love. Actually, Robinson does not, as charged, condone premarital sexual experience. His emphasis is upon approaching the problem in the spirit of love rather than law.

Again, situation ethics is largely a methodology of ethics. As such, it will undoubtedly serve as a stimulus for some serious and much-needed research in the area of the methodology of ethics. Here is an area of ethics, particularly Christian ethics, that demands, in the light of the radical social change of our century, some solid research. The confusion that reigns in contemporary moral life is, to some extent, due to a lack of understanding the basis of moral authority, the central ethical imperatives, and how moral decisions are to be made in concrete situations. A long step toward clarification of these issues is the development of a correct methodology in ethics.

Professional counselors and concerned pastors are especially appreciative of the situationalist's emphasis upon the new casuistry and the need for beginning with persons with problems rather than with prefabricated moral laws. From the standpoint of pastoral psychology, Seward Hiltner is enthusiastic about Fletcher's notion of "neocasuistry." Hiltner is right in noting that in "rejecting one kind of casuistry, Protestantism impeded any kind of 'case' approach, which pastoral care and pastoral psychology have finally got around to."[44] There are signs now of renewed interest in Richard Baxter's *The Christian Directory* and some concern for a Protestant casuistry. No doubt Fletcher's approach will provide impetus toward a more realistic Protestant study of casuistry.

Finally, the works of Robinson and Fletcher will serve as catalysts for a more serious study of Christian ethics by laymen. Teachers of Christian ethics are always a bit miffed when their discipline is identified in the popular mind with etiquette! Perhaps the situationists may serve to stimulate more study of Christian ethics in depth.

2. *Shortcomings of the Situationists*

Exponents of situation ethics betray certain basic weaknesses. Already in popular magazines and scholarly journals numerous articles are appearing condemning and praising the "new morality." Some pieces reflect more emotion than elucidation, more condemnation than comprehension. Here we shall attempt to bring the more constructive criticisms to bear upon the situationists.

Bultmann speaks of the "standardless moment" of moral decision. But he cannot escape the use of at least one "principle"—that of loving one's neighbor "as thyself." He assumes, erroneously, that everyone knows how to love in keeping with this moral imperative. What he throws out of the front door— ethical principles—he bootlegs in the back door. His assumption that every man "knows what is good" is, to say the least, highly questionable. His view of love tends toward subjectivism, and his concept of the "moment" is constantly in danger of becoming an abstraction.

Robinson and Fletcher lay themselves open to several valid criticisms. There is ambiguity with reference to the use by both of them of the terms "situation" and "love." One is never certain what they mean by these terms. To lay all stress upon love in the "right situation" is to talk about an abstraction, to raise an issue that is nonexistent. Just what the right situation may be is never described with any factuality.

The word "love" is also confusing as used by the situationists. Nowhere do they describe in a systematic fashion their various uses of love. As James Gustafson notes specifically in the case of Fletcher, love refers to everything he wants it to mean: the intrinsically good, justice, principle, disposition, ruling norm, etc.[45]

Both Robinson and Fletcher give priority to love, but they do so at the expense of the content of love. Love is the fulfillment of the law, but it does not abrogate the law. Love goes beyond the law, and is a higher order of morality for Christians. Paul provides content to love by pointing out that love of neighbor involves the principles of the Decalogue relating to conduct toward neighbor. "The commandments, 'You shall not commit adultery, You shall not kill, You shall not steal, You shall not covet,' and any other commandment, are summed up in this sentence, 'You shall love your neighbor as yourself.' Love does no wrong to a neighbor; therefore love is the fulfilling of the law." (Rom. 13: 9–10; cf. Mark 12:29 ff.; Gal. 5:14.)

It is true that both Robinson and Fletcher recognize some need for laws and principles. Robinson appears to accept the law at one end and to deny it at the other. At times he is a proponent of "rule-agapism" and at other times "act-agapism."[46] Fletcher declares that love plus the situation makes for right action. But then he speaks of love as a principle and as using its head. It appears that Robinson and Fletcher want to eat their ethical cake and have it too!

Both Robinson and Fletcher tend to equate the moral law with ecclesiastical law. The law forbidding David and other nonpriestly persons from eating "the bread of the Presence" appears to be as sacrosanct as laws about adultery, murder, and lying.[47] Certainly rules of religion must be set aside to meet human need, but they are not the moral law. Just because such ecclesiastical regulations were set aside by Jesus does not mean that all moral law is to be discarded when it is convenient to do so.

"Love alone," or situation ethics, is characterized by a one-sided methodology in arriving at moral decisions. It is a misplaced emphasis, a false polarization in Christian ethics. James Gustafson, of Yale Divinity School, has convincingly written that the umbrella named "contexualism" or "situationism" has become so large that it covers persons whose views are as different and divergent as some of the defenders of the "principles" approach.[48] He shows that Christian ethics begins from at least four points (situational, principle, theological, and relation to Jesus Christ), and regardless of which one is primary for the Christian ethicist, he moves toward the other three in the extension of his ethical posture with a Christian frame of reference.[49]

All emphasis upon extreme cases, the exception in Christian ethics, plays down the rule, limits ethical perspective, and often determines the moral answer before the existential moment of decision. For example, in 1804 at a logrolling near Louisville, Kentucky, the question arose as to whether or not a man would be justified in telling a falsehood under certain circumstances. This illustration was proposed: "Suppose a man has five children. The Indians come and kill four of them, the fifth one being hidden nearby. The savages then ask the father if he has another child, would he be justified in telling them that he had not?" The dispute waxed hot and finally got into the Long Run Baptist Church and split it into the "lying" and the "no-lying" Baptist churches![50]

Situation ethicists would, in the above situation, hold that the most loving act would be to lie and save the life of the child. Hence, the moral decision is determined before the ethical problem arises, a flat contradiction of their contention that prior moral decisions must not be made until the existential situation presents itself. Each situation is different and the individual is to do the will of God as it is revealed to him in the moment of decision. Under God, in this instance, the right act may be to say nothing or to refuse to reveal the whereabouts of the hidden child. There could be alternatives, but the situationists dogmatically decide beforehand what the moral decision is to be, namely, to lie and save the child.

Both Robinson and Fletcher are "act-utilitarian" (acting in the way that will likely produce the greatest balance of good over evil) when they move from personal to social relations. Fletcher states that when the love ethic seeks a social policy, it must form a coalition with utilitarianism, taking over from Bentham and Mill the principle of "The greatest good of the greatest number." However, in the coalition, agapē replaces the pleasure principle, the hedonistic calculus becomes the agapeic calculus. Happiness is doing the will of God, and utility sets the Christian to seeking his own happiness by seeking his neighbor's good on the widest possible scale.[51]

Fletcher clearly resorts to the principle of utility rather than revelation to relate love to social action. He does this because he knows that it is impossible to derive all our duties in the larger social life from love alone. And he must be aware of the fact that it is as difficult to derive what is the just thing to do from utility as it is from love. Christian theologians from

Thomas Aquinas to Emil Brunner have confronted this problem and have found no easy solution.

Finally, situationists tend to lack theological breadth and depth. Robinson's God is too small, too restricted to provide an adequate dynamic for his love ethic. God may be the "Ground of our Being," but he also has other dimensions—"out there," "up here," and "under there," as well as "in here." God cannot be packaged in the neat definition of "Ground of Being." Noticeably absent in Fletcher is any serious concern for repentance, judgment, human nature, and redemption. Robinson leaves the impression that modern man is grown up and therefore has little need for spiritual help outside of himself.

Robinson betrays a naïve view of sin. He admits that there is a whole class of actions (stealing, lying, killing, and adultery) that are so destructive of human relations that no differences of time or society can change their character.[52] But this does not mean that in certain circumstances these could never be right. Yet, he has no answer to the questions of rape and incest. Can they ever be justified by motives, circumstances, and consequences?

C. TOWARD A MORE REALISTIC MORALITY

Situationism is a needed corrective for overemphasis upon laws, codes, rules, and principles. But it is not a self-sufficient methodology in Christian ethics. Hence, the corrective stands in need of a corrective, for it is too limited a system. The Christian ethic is so rich and varied that it is not a matter of either the freedom and ultimacy of pure act-agapism or pure rule-agapism.[53] Christian ethics involves both *agapē and principles* for its completion. That *agapē* indicates certain norms of behavior, general principles that embody its own nature, may be seen in its qualities and in the statements of what it demands (I Cor., ch. 13). Principles do not restrain the freedom of love, but provide concreteness and fulfillment in Christian action. Principle-agapism furnishes content and guidelines for the direction that love may take in concrete situations.

Hence, principle-agapism saves Christian ethics from the twin perils of legalism and antinomianism. It takes into account the situation and seeks the most loving norms of action.

To rule out general principles of conduct in Christian ethics is to limit the freedom of love in determining the right, to impose too heavy a burden upon the conscience in decision making, and to disregard the past accumulated moral wisdom of the Christian faith.[54]

It appears to this writer that Christian ethics can remain contextual without dispensing with principles. As has been noted, Bultmann, Robinson, and Fletcher are unable to dispense with principles altogether. Bultmann admits that they are helpful precipitates out of past experience, though the decision of the moment is never determined by such knowledge. "Decision is not dice-throwing," he says, and its character is clearer when practical possibilities are understood.[55] As indicated above, he makes love of neighbor "as thyself" a universal principle. Robinson declares that the link "between bed and board, between sex and the sharing of life at every level, must be pressed as strongly as ever."[56] This is, in fact, a statement of principle. Fletcher's act-agapism drives toward principles by falling back upon reason, "neocasuistry," and the summary rule as truths to be discerned by the Christian in decision making.

Hence, there is no escape from the use of principles in Christian ethics. The Christian brings to the situation not only his awareness of redemption, Biblical ethical wisdom, and common sense but also the general objectives of order, freedom, truth, and concern as guides to prevent decisions from being blind. Love-embodying principles can serve in an advisory, if not always definitive, role in moral decisions.[57]

There is more—the function of the Holy Spirit in moral decisions, a sadly neglected factor by almost all Christian ethicists.[58] Yet the fruit of the Spirit is presented in ethical terms: love, joy, peace, patience, kindness, goodness, faithfulness, gentleness, self-control (Gal. 5:22-23). Christian character and hope are made possible "because God's love has been poured into our hearts through the Holy Spirit which has been given to us" (Rom. 5:5). Without the energizing and enabling power of the Spirit, the Christian ethic is impossible. For it is the Spirit who ultimately informs the Christian in concrete moral decisions and guides him "into all the truth" (John 16:13).

III. THE NEW SEX CODE:
"PERMISSIVENESS WITH AFFECTION"

ATTITUDES toward sex are radically changing in American society. So drastic are these changes that some people even speak of a "sexplosion" and "revolution in sexual ethics." Certainly ours is a "sex-saturated" and "sex-affirming" society in which there has been an erosion of the traditional sex code of chastity before and after marriage. Commenting upon the Kinsey Report, realist Reinhold Niebuhr has declared that we are "approaching the license which characterized Roman civilization in the period of its decay."[1]

Allegedly this is the second sexual revolution our country has witnessed, the first occurring after World War I with the appearance of the "jazz age." But there are basic differences. Parents, during the first sexual revolution, had a code against sexual sins and knew that these sins were wrong. Now their children are adrift upon a sea of permissiveness with a code expressed by Ernest Hemingway: "What is moral is what you feel good after, and what is immoral is what you feel bad after."[2] Consequently, the present generation of young people sees little wrong in premarital sexual relations.

A. SEX ATTITUDES AND STANDARDS
IN AMERICAN SOCIETY

At least five views of sex prevail in our nation today: (1) There is the Puritanical view, which holds that sex is nasty, unmentionable, and taboo. (2) The Freudian view of sex advocates the theory that neurosis is the result of repressed sexual impulses. The popularized version of Freudianism is one of the strong forces that helped to break down the Puritan view of sex. (3) There is the deification of sex as the ultimate in life by such writers as D. H. Lawrence. (4) The *Playboy* view of sex, as advocated by Hugh Hefner, says that sex is a bodily function which man shares with animals. It is like eating and drinking, a physical demand that must be satisfied. And (5) there is the traditional Christian view, which holds that sex is good but can be abused. Its purpose is for procreation and the expression of tender love within wedlock.

Several sex standards prevail in our culture. These are: (1) the formal standard or the single standard of abstinence on the part of the unmarried; (2) the informal or double standard, which insists that premarital sexual experience is wrong for all women, but excusable, if not right, for all men;[3] and (3) there is the permissive standard, a pattern now evolving as revealed in the Kinsey and similar reports.

Hence we have moved from a single, Puritanical standard of abstinence, into a double standard, and are now in the process of leaving these behind for an era of permissiveness and "free love" in sexual relations.

B. CAUSATIVE FACTORS IN CHANGING SEX CODES

Contributing factors to our changing attitudes toward sex are numerous. For one thing, there has been a loss of religious authority and a lessening of respect for religious teaching on sex. The traditional attitude of the church toward sex—that is, that sex is evil—the disparagement of marriage, and the rise of asceticism, all of which are negative, have given rise to new attitudes toward sex and a rebellion against the teachings of the church on sex.[4]

Further, there was the contribution of the romantic type of love, the cult of romantic passion, holding that true love could exist only outside of marriage. It was driven underground by the church, but reappeared in the early twentieth century in a new form. The influence of Freud has already been mentioned. His interpreters contend that repression of the natural sexual instincts at several stages of development may likely lead to neurosis. Hence, the exponents of "free love" discovered a psychological sanction for their behavior.

The philosophy of individualism—that what one does is his own business—has become popular with the masses. Throwing off all restraints, young people are declaring their freedom now in sex matters. Adults are going along, lost in an orgy of open-mindedness so characteristic of the times. Hence, they have no sort of specific guidance in sex matters for their offspring.

Abstinence has been losing its adherents because of the invention of new and easily secured methods for the prevention of pregnancy. The pill and cheap contraceptives have reduced the risk of pregnancy. Social condemnation along with guilt feelings has all but faded from the American scene. Some counselors and therapists who see positive values in premarital experiences advise parents to accept lenient attitudes toward premarital intercourse.

Sociological factors, such as World Wars I and II, industrialization, and commercialization have taken their toll in the breaking down of traditional sex codes. Prolonged periods of living abroad on the part of military men in the atmosphere of imminent death, away from home ties and restraints, have encouraged sexual freedom.[5]

Industrialization has helped to emancipate woman, taking her out of the home and increasing social and professional contacts between herself and men. It has provided the automobile, which some people regard as a powerful influence on teen-age conduct with reference to sexual behavior. Then came the motel, which provides a rendezvous for sexual intercourse that was not available a generation ago.[6]

Commercialization of sex has become an accepted practice in American society. Perfume, hair tonics, and such are portrayed as both seductive and dangerous. Nudity and flagrantly suggestive slogans have become standard methods utilized by advertising agencies. Also under the guise of "art," the American public has been inundated with "sexiness" via the media of films, television, stage, and literature. Some of this actually deifies sex, reminiscent of the ancient worship of Venus. It would appear that sexuality is exploited by these pseudo artists to compensate for a lack of genuine artistic talent. But more practically (and thus, it seems, more importantly) sex sells! Hence, the hearty endorsement from Madison Avenue.

These and other factors have precipitated the sexual revolution in this country. Clearly, sexuality is in crisis. Hence, there is a search for new sex codes in a changing society. Old philosophies and patterns of sex are reappearing under new guises.

There is the so-called "new morality" concept that one should live by "permissiveness with affection." Ira Reiss sets forth the basic tenets of this view: (1) morals are a private affair; (2) being in love justifies premarital sex, and by implication extramarital sex; and (3) nothing is really wrong as long as nobody gets hurt.[7]

Some people advocate "little marriages" before the big one. This is recommended by an American minister who does not want to be quoted.[8] "Serial polygamy," that is, a succession of love affairs with legal approval, is becoming acceptable in America. Likewise, the European pattern is becoming popular. This system supports the view that infidelity in marriage does not demand a divorce, because it may help the family to remain together.

C. THE *PLAYBOY* PHILOSOPHY

Perhaps the most popular view of sex in America today is that which is advocated in the *Playboy* Philosophy of Hugh Hefner. After Hefner left the military service, he was married, had two children, was divorced, failed as a cartoonist and as a copywriter for *Esquire* magazine, and seemed to be vanishing into oblivion. But then he got the big idea. He secured the copyrights for a nude shot of Marilyn Monroe, illustrated a few jokes, borrowed six thousand dollars, sold some stock, and produced *Playboy* magazine in 1953.[9]

Hefner has built an empire on sex. At thirty-nine, he lives in his forty-eight room $800,000 Chicago palace. Here he lives in Hefnerland with his "special girl" and two dozen others working in the Hefner empire. In the three rooms he has allocated for himself, Hefner works, choosing all cartoons and photographs and directing the $70,000,000 Hefner enterprise.

Son of devout Methodist parents, Hefner appears to have little appreciation for the church. According to him, through the centuries the church has emphasized sex primarily as sin, and in the most extreme form of the Puritanism that has so influenced our Anglo-Saxon culture. The result of this heritage is a society that is fearful, suspicious, and confused about sex. In an attempt to liberate society, Hefner presents his *Playboy* Philosophy. Simply stated, this philosophy is:

> Sex is a function of the body, a drive which man shares with the animals. Like eating, drinking, and sleeping, it is a physical demand that must be satisfied. If you don't satisfy it, you will have all sorts of neuroses and repression psychoses. Sex is here to stay. Let's forget the prudery that makes us hide from it. Throw away those inhibitions, find a girl who is like-minded and let yourself go.[10]

The Playboy is not a bum, but rather a man who is sensitive to pleasure and is intent on proving his masculinity. Hefner himself sets the example. He is "happily unmarried." He feels that neither the church nor the government should interfere with private, intimate subjects such as sex.[11] He contends that the Declaration of Independence proclaims the right of every citizen to life, liberty, and the pursuit of happiness.[12] Adultery, therefore, is the private business of the people involved.[13] Moreover, he declares: "We agree that sex can be both enjoyable and beautiful, but the suggestion that *all* sex outside of marriage is ugly and not enjoyable is absurd, and as unreasoned as would be the suggestion that *all* sex inside of marriage is joyful and beautiful."[14]

Hefner holds that divorce should be by mutual consent. If there are any children in a marriage, a period of counseling should precede any divorce action. But if this fails, a divorce should be allowed. We live in a society, he contends, where trial marriage is a way of life. We may pretend "to live in a monogamous society, but a great many of us are practicing what has been called 'sequential polygamy.' "[15]

What is needed in this country are, believes Hefner, stricter marriage laws, so that there will not be so many early marriages. It follows that couples should be allowed to have sexual relations before they are married. This will cause them to wait longer and to be more certain about compatibility. When they do get married, they will be better adjusted, and there will be fewer divorces and less unhappiness.[16]

As for homosexuality, Hefner confesses that he has a strong personal prejudice in favor of the boy-girl variety of sex. But he thinks that in our free, rational, and human society there should be a tolerance of those who find their sexual satisfaction in other ways, so long as their activity does not involve minors and is limited to consenting adults. His position is: "I'm not prejudiced against homosexuals, but I wouldn't want my brother to marry one."[17]

For promulgating the *Playboy* Philosophy, Hefner has developed some ingenious techniques. There is the *Playboy* magazine, which will sell three million copies a month and gross twenty-eight million dollars this year (1965).[18]

Playboy is a good magazine, according to journalistic standards. It attracts the top names in advertising, especially the big liquor manufacturers. It pays up to three thousand dollars for lead articles, fifteen hundred dollars for others. It features Round Table discussions with outstanding pastors, rabbis, and priests, the results of which are reprinted and sent to religious leaders and teachers. Also, there are interviews with celebrities in the entertainment world, in art, and in music. The magazine also features jokes, fiction, nude photographs, and articles on cars, cheese, clothing, vacations, financial matters, art, and a host of other subjects that appeal to the "sophisticated, *avant-garde* male."

There is also the *Playboy* Advisor, who answers questions of varied nature. There is also the *Playboy* Forum, which is an interchange of ideas between reader and editor on subjects raised by the *Playboy* Philosophy. Some ministers write in expressing appreciation for certain aspects of Hefner's "philosophy." A "*Playboy* Sermon" appears in the March, 1965, issue of *Playboy* Forum, in which the minister agrees with some of Hefner's basic views.[19]

Perhaps the most famous feature of *Playboy* magazine is its monthly foldout photo of a "playmate." She is usually nude or near nude. She adorns the dorm walls of thousands of college students as a pinup girl. She is the symbol of the woman who has casual and satisfying sexual experiences with a successful single young man or an unhappily married man. She knows her place and the rules of the game and requires nothing more.

Who reads *Playboy?* The young man on the way up, and up on what he is down on; the *Playboy* reader is a masterful mixer who prefers being sold on a brand before he buys. He lives with the best of spirits: 86.1 percent of all *Playboy* households drink or serve alcoholic beverages. Above all, what Hefner believes in is the individual. Declares Hefner: "What we believe in, first and foremost, is the individual—and his right to be an individual. If a man has a right to find God in his own way, he has a right to go to the Devil in his own way, also. . . . The Bible singles out the meek and the poor in spirit for special blessings. We'd like to add one of our own: Blessed is the rebel—without him there would be no progress."[20]

Another means of propagating the *Playboy* Philosophy is the *Playboy* Club or Bunny Club. Members have *Playboy* credit cards and keys. In addition, there are *Playboy* hotels, Playmates, and accessories such as *Playboy* sweaters, ankle bracelets, earrings, pendants, pins, bracelets, cuff links, lighters, cards, towels, coffee and beer mugs, perfume, and wallets.

Any critique of Hefner's views of sex involves both pro and con elements. His insistence that there are inconsistencies in our marriage laws is well taken, along with the need for stricter and more uniform marriage laws. Marriage parlors should go, and marriage should be interpreted as an adult enterprise. His view that marriage is not for procreation alone is significant. Marriage is also for the expression of tender love. His charge that the church has said little that is positive about the sex life of the single person should challenge it to engage in a program of sex education for all members. The *Playboy* Philosophy attracts adherents because it offers discussions on and answers (such as they are) to many questions of a sexual nature—an area our churches have been content to gloss over with a pious veneer of moralism.

On the con side, it must be said that Hefner has commercialized sex in a subtle and sophisticated manner. There is money in the exploitation of sex, and Hefner is getting his share of it. He avoids the crude and unsophisticated pornography that itself has become a half-billion-dollar business.

Playboy Philosophy is basically egocentric. Hefner's hyper-individualism is reflected in almost every article he writes. His guiding principle is that of "enlightened self-interest," which becomes a dogma of his philosophy. To be concerned with one's interests and happiness is both right and natural. Hefner finds a sanction for his selfishness by noting that man and lower animals are primarily motivated by self-interest. Hefner attempts to make his view respectable by implying that it is, after all, good old American "rugged individualism." Perhaps he is not aware of it, but this position makes him a bedfellow of the rabid fundamentalist in religion.

In fairness to Hefner, he does insist that the individual should be concerned for the welfare of others, especially the less fortunate. But he leaves one with the distinct impression that what is good for Hefner as an individual is good for the country. Thus he advocates the old fallacy that everyone pursuing his own interests will somehow benefit society as a whole.[21]

Playboy Philosophy claims to liberate from Puritanical views of sex. In actuality, it is a new form of tyranny. The "liberated" find themselves in bondage to the latest word from Hefner as to what to consume and what is proper behavior for the orthodox playboy.

Again, the *Playboy* view of reality desacralizes sex and reduces it to a casual commodity for human consumption. For Hefner, sex is neither sacred nor profane. Rather, it is a natural, neutral thing to be enjoyed by any man or woman who feels the urge.[22] This is to completely depersonalize sex and to make it merely a packageable item to meet a physical need much as a glass of water for a thirsty man. Sex, for Hefner, is just another ingredient in *Playboy*'s "total entertainment and service package for the young urban male."[23]

Hefner's philosophy is only a partial presentation of the facts of life. His literature does not reveal the tragic things that happen to those who practice its teachings. Since he portrays only the glamour and the gaiety of the *Playboy* way of life, he is propagating a half-truth. What happens to his "special girl," his personal playbunny, when he has used her for his own pleasure? The answer is that of disillusionment. One of his ex-girls, who began going to a psychiatrist as her relation with Hefner tapered off, is reported to have declared: "Sometimes—God, I don't feel like I have any identity of my own."[24] One might also hope that Hefner would run some factual stories in his magazine about playboys and playbunnies when they arrive at middle age or past fifty.

Hefner and his *Playboy* Philosophy have no sense of social responsibility. Divorce is to be by mutual consent regardless of what happens to the children. This is a basically selfish and irresponsible position. No one with any sensitivity for the needs of children could advocate such a crude view.

Playboy Philosophy trivializes sex. Hefner starts with the premise that sex is the pleasure of the moment, like the ice-cream cone, and consequently yields only a momentary pleasure. Sex is reduced to a mere reflex action.[25]

Because Hefner removes the personal dimension from sex, it is reduced to the animal level. In this view, sex is to be casual and impersonal with no entanglements. Animals act by instinct in sexuality and he advocates that men do the same with anyone who is willing to go along.

Finally, Hefner has no place for the Biblical view of faithful love. Fidelity is one of the basic foundations of marriage. Chastity before and after marriage is the demand of the Christian ethic. Without fidelity, marriage is usually dissolved or at least becomes an intolerable relationship.

D. FRUITS OF THE NEW FREEDOM

The false freedom advocated by Hefner and others contributes to the current tragedy in American sexual relations. In spite of widespread knowledge of birth control, the rates of illegitimate births are high. Approximately two hundred and fifty thousand babies are born out of wedlock each year in the United States. It is estimated that one out of every five American brides is pregnant at the time of marriage. Kinsey and subsequent studies reveal that the majority of American men and half the women have sexual intercourse before marriage.[26] Infidelity in marriage relations is high, with one half of the husbands and one fourth of the wives engaging in extramarital sexual relations.

The high incidence of venereal diseases continues, about two hundred thousand cases per year. From two hundred thousand to one million illegal abortions are performed in the United States each year.[27]

Sexual intercourse before marriage and its consequences are reported in numerous studies. According to Dr. Blaine, the psychiatrist to Harvard and Radcliffe Health Service, over the past fifteen years premarital intercourse among boys prior to graduation rose from 50 to 60 percent, the number of college girls from 25 to 40 percent.[28] More and more college youth no longer consider the loss of virginity an "American Tragedy."[29]

E. SOME CHRISTIAN APPROACHES TO SEX

The sexual revolution has stimulated various efforts on the part of theologians to meet its challenge. Exponents of the so-called "new morality" emphasize the primacy of love in contrast to prescriptive morality, persons instead of principles, in dealing with sex problems. They argue that any action can be an expression of love in the right situation. Reacting to this position are those who insist upon the deductive method of applying Biblical proof texts and traditional absolutes to premarital and extramarital relations, holding that such action is always wrong.

1. Advocates of the New Sexual Morality

Among Christian thinkers who advocate love without law in dealing with sexuality is Bishop John A. T. Robinson, who insists that in dealing with premarital sex one should not begin with the law that states that fornication is always wrong. Rather, one should start with love, a deep concern for persons as whole persons in their total social context. He provides an example of what he means. If a young man asks, "Why shouldn't I have sexual relations with a girl?" it is easy to answer, "Because it is wrong" or, "Because it is a sin" and then condemn him. Rather, one should ask and answer the question, "Do you love her?" or, "How much do you love her?" and then help him "to accept *for himself* the decision that, if he doesn't, or doesn't very deeply, then his action is immoral, or, if he does, then he will respect her far too much to use her or take liberties with her."[30] Then Robinson states the principle of the whole matter by saying: "Chastity is the expression of charity —of caring, enough. And this is the criterion for every form of behaviour, inside marriage or out of it, in sexual ethics or in any other field."[31]

Hence, Robinson wants a morality of freedom from the "Thou shalt not" approach to sex problems, for young people ask "Why?" and want a basis for morality that makes sense in

personal relations. Chastity is honesty in sex, not just abstinence.[32]

Another Anglican, Canon Douglas Rhymes, follows essentially the same approach as Robinson in dealing with sex problems. He reports being asked by a young man why he shouldn't
have sex with his steady girl friend if she were willing?
Rhymes's answer was a series of questions designed to sensi-
tize the boy to a sense of responsibility. He asked whether the
boy planned to marry the girl and pointed out that if something went wrong, she would suffer more than he. Then
Rhymes added:

> If you tell me that you love her, then I would say to you that
> sex is not isolated from love, but part of love and that, if you
> say you love someone, you care for her body, mind and spirit;
> you do not treat her as simply the instrument for your own de-
> sires. That would mean that you attach no value to her, and very
> little to yourself.[33]

Finally, Rhymes told the youth that "no one could really
answer his question but himself, but that these were the kinds
of questions he must be putting to himself."[34]

H. A. Williams, dean of Trinity College, Cambridge, believes that sexual intercourse outside marriage is not always
wrong. Examples are taken from two recent movies. In the first
is a portrayal of how a nervous sailor achieves confidence in
himself through the way a prostitute gives herself to him.
"What is seen," declares Williams, "is an act of charity which
proclaims the glory of God. . . . He [the sailor] goes away a
deeper fuller person than he came in." The second film depicts
how a man, strongly attracted to small girls and a menace to
them, finds the courage to go to bed with an older woman.
After sleeping together, he is "made whole." Williams adds:
"And where there is healing, there is Christ, whatever the
Church may say about fornication. And the appropriate response is—Glory to God in the Highest."[35]

In this country, Joseph Fletcher proposes a sex ethic based

on love rather than law, in which the ultimate criterion for right and wrong is based upon the individual's subjective perception of what is good for himself and his neighbor in each given situation. The core of the matter is that "there is only one thing which is always good regardless of circumstances, and that is neighborly concern, social responsibility, *agape*—which is a divine imperative."[36]

In the situational approach of the new morality, Fletcher is quoted in *Time* as saying that "one enters into every decision-making moment armed with all the wisdom of culture, but prepared in one's freedom to suspend and violate any rule except that one must as responsibly as possible seek the good of one's neighbor."[37] To this the writer of the article adds that this "is quite a long thought for an eighteen-year-old during a passionate moment in the back seat of a car."[38]

All the above exponents of the new morality frown upon a scheme of "codified conduct" and emphasize the primacy of love. In each situation nothing is prescribed except love. All laws, rules, and commands against sexual promiscuity are ruled out. Obviously this is highly subjective and assumes that everyone knows what the New Testament means by *agapē*. Clearly they do not. Robinson himself declares that the new ethic is "highly dangerous," but that it is the only ethic for "man come of age."[39] Besides, has man really "come of age" and is he capable of living without laws and principles? Modern man may have conquered much in science and space, but he has not yet been able to overcome his sinful nature fully.

On the positive side, Robinson and those of his persuasion are to be commended for their emphasis upon dealing with persons as persons in concrete situations. But they tend to ignore social responsibility, and there is little emphasis upon sexual promiscuity as a violation of God's will in human sexual relations.

2. Answers to the New Morality

Exponents of the new sexual morality have not gone unchallenged. Dr. Paul Ramsey, of Princeton University, at a meeting at Harvard Divinity School in 1965 of five hundred ministers and educators gathered to discuss the sexual aspects of the new morality, had some pertinent observations to make about this matter. He declared that the Christian ethic involves a view of marital relations so deeply rooted in the need of persons for the *unitive* that it can be justified only within the marriage relationship of a lifelong commitment.[40] He went on to say that the new morality could not ignore the divinely given link between sexual relations and procreation.[41]

Elsewhere Ramsey spells out in detail his position.[42] He notes that a true "situationist" in his ethics "should stress the fact that an act of sexual love is still a procreative act" and that he should not forget that there is the danger of venereal disease that may affect any child born of the sexual act.[43]

Ramsey further observes that couples engaged to be married who contemplate premarital sexual relations in the authentic moral meaning of this phrase know that they are seeking to justify something that is not fully responsible. Moreover, they know that they are taking more and offering less than love requires. Hence, they can only attempt to act as if they were married.[44]

Richard A. McCormick, S.J., makes a strong case for the absoluteness of moral imperatives in relation to sexuality.[45] He shows the danger of the severing of sex from the human context. "Once there is autonomy," he notes, "there is depersonalization and decontextualization of human sexuality."[46] And depersonalized sex is simply inhuman. At this point, the new morality is blind to the fact that absolute moral imperatives do not abandon the personalist structure of genuine personal, authentic, and responsible relationships. On the contrary, these imperatives affirm the sacredness of these relationships. He admits that traditional prohibitions are negative, but that they are asserting "a value and significance for sexual acts, and that it is precisely this value which is compromised by their violation."[47]

McCormick concludes that the new morality is, above all, a struggle to recover the significance of sex. While the traditional Biblical and church teachings of fornication and adultery may be meaningless to modern man, they may but suggest our clouded vision of the values of the old norms.[48]

Robert Fitch, dean of the Pacific School of Religion, Berkeley, California, offers a "commonsense sex code," devised primarily for young people vulnerable to the accommodation of the new morality.[49] While he affirms the primacy of love, he does not see it as a "dangling emotion without organic connection to the larger realms of thought, feeling and action which makes us whole as human beings."[50] He does not think that it is charity to teach that one can be a person without having principles.

Either you control sex, says Fitch, or it controls you. It is inconsistent to tell youth that they must curb their appetites for food, drink, and tobacco and not to tell them the same thing about sex. Sex may control one by forcing him into parenthood or marriage or a job before he is ready to accept them.

Moreover, Fitch says that sex is for human beings, and this means that it must be blended with intelligence and love. But many human beings are using sex as do animals. Sex is social because it has a social outcome in terms of babies and the dimensions of vocational, economic, civil, political, aesthetic, and religious relationships. Sex is for persons. It is an ultimate evil to depersonalize sex, for it cannot be cut off from its organic relationship to affection and the social order, requiring regulation and control.[51]

Fitch is to be commended in that he takes sex problems seriously and emphasizes the personal and social aspects of sexual relations. His development of a simple, commonsense code for sexuality will appeal to many. However, his code may be too simple, for he fails to show how in a positive way man can control his sex life. Also, there is no direct theological substance to his code. He fails to make mention of Christ and omits any reference to divine aid or guidance.

Seward Hiltner attempts to base his approach to sexual morality upon Biblical and psychological foundations.[52] Hence, he relies upon the Biblical and the developmental principles of understanding sex. He states that since man is a whole being, sex is good if it serves the fulfillment of man as a total being; that is, if it serves God's will for man.[53] Also, he stresses the need for fidelity in the Christian view of sex as against sentimental and idealistic views of sex. Hiltner makes it clear that good and evil in sex can be known only in the light of the love and judgment of God.

F. TOWARD A THEOLOGY OF SEXUALITY

A constructive response to the problem of sex must take seriously the Biblical view of sexuality, its theological interpretation, and the response of the church. Only the barest outline of these factors can be treated here. But the salient elements of a theologically oriented ethic of sex can be suggested.

1. Key Concepts in the Biblical View of Sex

Rather than attempt a systematic presentation of the Old and New Testament teachings on sexuality, we are choosing certain pivotal concepts that are essential to an understanding of the Christian view of sex.

First, there is the "one flesh" principle of sexual relations (Gen. 2:24; Matt. 19:5; Mark 10:7; I Cor. 6:16; Eph. 5:31). The Genesis account states: "Therefore a man leaves his father and his mother and cleaves to his wife, and they become one flesh" (Gen. 2:24). This is a union based upon sexual relations between a man and a woman. But this unitive experience is more than a physical one. When "two become one flesh" it involves a complete union, including the sexual. D. S. Bailey notes that the "one flesh" describes "the essential informing principle in marriage, the interior, ontological aspect of sexual union."[54] Therefore, a true institutional marriage is the formal expression of the mysterious *henōsis* (union, becoming one) by a man and a woman in consummating their love.[55]

The "one flesh" relation is a revelation of self-identity. Adam and Eve were originally one flesh and they had to come together again to discover what it meant to be man and woman. Sexuality is a gift of God that drives man and woman together to overcome their isolation, fragmentation, and self-centeredness. In the experience of mutual self-giving, Adam and Eve achieved self-awareness and self-identity.

The Biblical term "to know" is used to designate the sexual act. But it is more than a mere euphemism confined to sexual intercourse. This verb is used both to denote a spiritual, personal relationship to God and for sexuality (Isa. 11:2; Jer. 22:16; Hos. 4:6; Gen. 4:1, 25; Judg. 19:25; cf. Matt. 1:25). Otto Piper claims that "to know" is used deliberately because in the sex act there is conveyed a genuine knowledge of one's self and of another, namely, the secret meaning of one's manhood and womanhood.[56] Hence, this knowledge is more than "the facts of life," the story of "the birds and the bees and the flowers." There is in sexual intercourse the mutual surrender of the depth of being. There is, in short, a communication in coitus of personhood.

While Jesus had little to say about sex per se, he does stress the "one flesh" union. With reference to the question of divorce, he takes it out of the realm of debate and harks back to God's divine intention of the marriage of one man and one woman in the "one flesh" relationship (Matt. 19:1–9; Mark 10:2–9). He makes it clear that the ideal of marriage brooks no grounds for severing the "one flesh" union.

Paul goes so far as to declare that a casual relation with a prostitute involves more than a physical act. (I Cor. 6:16.) In contradiction to the argument that fornication is a "natural" function of the body, just as eating and drinking, the apostle claims that coitus in or out of marriage establishes the state of "one flesh." "Do you not know," he says, "that he who joins himself to a prostitute becomes one body with her? For, as it is written, 'The two shall become one.'" (I Cor. 6:16.) Here Paul is affirming that the sexual embrace, no matter how detached, casual, or commercial, involves the total personality. Note that Paul uses the word "body" (sōma), the total self. "Intercourse therefore," as Bailey states, "is much more than a mere physical act. . . . It involves and affects the whole man and the whole woman in the very centre and depth of their being, so that afterwards neither can ever be as if they had never come together."[57] Hence, there can be no casual, "natural," or promiscuous sexual intercourse without affecting the total person.

"Love" (*agapē*) is another key term in an adequate understanding of the Biblical view of sexuality. Biblical *agapē* is "existence-for-the-other-person" as manifested in the life and teaching of Jesus Christ. His care and concern for the church is the model for the husband-wife relationship. (Eph. 5:21–33.) Christ loves and sacrifices himself for his bride, the church. He is "Savior," that is, not only redeemer, but also preserver, sustainer, and guardian of the church. Likewise, husbands are to love their wives in the same manner. This "bridal theology" is not original with the apostle. The metaphor of marriage is a profound symbol of God's relation to his people in both the Old and the New Testaments. (Hosea; Rev. 19:7–9; 21:2–10.) With Paul, the metaphor becomes normative for Christian marriage. How can anyone conclude that Paul presents a degrading view of marriage after reading Eph. 5:21–33? For here the most exalted view of marriage in history is held before the world.

It should be stressed that agapeic love does not take the place of sexual love. Rather, *agapē* takes *erōs* (human love) into its service and leads one to love the other sexually just as one does in any other way.[58] Christian love recognizes the essential and rightful place of sexual love, transforms it, and gives it true meaning. *Agapē* is the love of God operating between husband and wife in all their relations, including the sexual. This kind of love finds expression in the husband-wife union in terms of kindness, concern, consideration, and justice.

2. The Case for Chastity

The ethical implications of the "one flesh" union and *agapē* should be clear. Sex in the Scriptures is not regarded as evil in itself, but as a God-given impulse that draws man and woman together into a "one flesh" union so that they overcome their solitude and establish their self-identity in community. Sexuality, therefore, is accepted as a gift from God, a great mystery. Hence, sex is surrounded by restrictions to protect its misuse. The Bible is replete with taboos and laws against homosexuality, incest, adultery, and fornication. Chastity before and after marriage is the norm of sexual relations.

Chastity in the Scriptures is grounded in creation, in the "one flesh" union. This indicates a monogamous pattern of marriage for life. (See Rom. 7:2–3.) Marriage for God's people, therefore, is to be holy, an example to the pagan world: "Let marriage be held in honor among all, and let the marriage bed be undefiled; for God will judge the immoral and the adulterous." (Heb. 13:4.) Adultery is the violation of the "one flesh" unity, the ontological aspect of marriage. The deep, hidden bond is irrevocably marred in extramarital sexual acts. William G. Cole says:

> Even idolatry can be undone and forgiven. But the sex act once committed with another person cannot be undone. The interpersonal relationship has undergone a radical change, and the couple involved can never return to where they were before. Something indelible has stamped them both. Even with a prostitute, sexual connection leaves its mark and its memory.[59]

Chastity is also grounded in the covenant of God with his people. This covenant in the Old Testament, depicted in the marriage metaphor, points to monogamy and exclusiveness. Israel's whoring after other gods is described as adultery and a violation of the covenant with his people and his exclusive claim upon their lives (Jer. 3:1–2; Hos. 5:3; 6:10). Likewise the New Testament, where the analogy of fornication and adultery is used in connection with the worship of false gods, points to fidelity and monogamy in married life (I Cor. 6:9–20; Eph. 5:5; Rev. 2:22).

Paul's metaphor in Eph., ch. 5, clearly indicates that Christian marriage is monogamic and exclusive. Purity in sex life is a witness to the Christian's loyalty to the model of love Christ demonstrates in his love for the church. Extramarital sex acts are a contradiction of the faithful love of Christ for his body, the church.

Finally, *agapē* implies chastity and monogamy in the marriage relationship. Helmut Thielicke observes that there is no "law" in the Scriptures that demands monogamy, but that under the gospel there is a *trend* in this direction and that it "becomes" the sole form of relationship.[60] He thinks that the motive for monogamy is *agapē*, which demands full acceptance of the other person. *Agapē* "causes the husband to deal with his wife as a unique, individual person and thus checks his own tendency toward polygamy."[61]

Human love itself tends toward monogamy and the desire for exclusive sexual relations between two persons. This is not to rule out the polygamous instinct, for it does exist. But persons who genuinely love each other "feel the intrusion of a third person to be intolerably disturbing, that a strong and genuine love—still quite apart from any idea of ethical obligation—does want the loved one wholly and solely for itself."[62] Such love always feels: "It is with this particular person that I wish to live alone and for always."[63] True human love is monistic in its very essence, focusing upon the one beloved to the exclusion of all others.

Beyond the Biblical demand for chastity before and after marriage, there are psychological and social arguments for it. Evelyn Duvall has spelled these out in popular but scholarly fashion.[64] She presents realistic and specific reasons for premarital chastity for today's youth. Among the many myths that she explodes are: "Everybody does it"; "It's natural"; "It's fun"; and "Sexual restraint is bad." Then she proceeds to show how premarital sexual relations affect marriage, family, and reputation.

3. The Role of the Church in Sex Education

The church has the greatest opportunity of any institution to strengthen moral quality in sexual relations. It possesses the resources, personnel, and a Christian philosophy of sexuality. Yet the church has failed to present a positive approach to sex. It certainly has a rationale for engaging in a program of sex education. Parents are finding it difficult to communicate with their children about sex problems. Studies show that most young people are reluctant to talk with parents about love, sex, and marriage.[65] The church has an opportunity and a responsibility to minister both to parents and to children in this situation.

Although an increasing number of "facts" about sexuality are appearing in the mass media, advice books, and popular magazines, much of the information is misleading and distorted.[66] There is still an enormous amount of misinformation about conception, pregnancy, birth, and sexual adjustment in marriage. Here the church can provide a sound sex education program from the perspective of the Christian faith.

A sex education program can be developed and administered by a local church. It is not my purpose here to suggest such a program in detail. Suffice it to say that any sex education in a church should include both parents and children. Competent leaders and adequate literature must be developed. Some worthwhile materials may be had from denominational headquarters. But literature that deals frankly and factually with sex will have to be secured from the specialists. Sex education in the churches must be aimed at every age level from the junior to the adult. It must take into account each stage of biological, emotional, and ethical development. Sex facts must be interpreted within the context of the essential needs of each age level.

Pastoral response to sexuality should be a positive one. With the situationists, the minister may begin with persons in trouble, where they are in concrete situations, not with the attitude of condemnation, but of redemptive purpose. In his redemptive efforts, the pastor will be equipped with the Christian perspective and scientific facts about sexuality. In addition, he will bring to the situation the Christian doctrines of repentance and forgiveness. Armed with these resources, he will do what is in keeping with love-embodying principles in each case. "Love alone" ethics is an inadequate approach to "man come of age" as he grapples with problems of sexuality. In attempting to avoid legalism, the radical situationists stress *agapē* without love-embodying principles, which may lead into the sand trap of subjectivism. If love is not defined in terms of objective ethical guidelines, such as chastity, charity, and concern for others, and grounded in the living Christ, it has no adequate dynamic and dissolves into sentimentality.

IV. THE NEW CHURCH:
"SERVANT IN A SECULAR SOCIETY"

THE CHURCH today is in confrontation with a whole complex of "isms." Cultural forces such as communism, materialism, scientism, naturalism, humanism, and secularism are rivals of the Christian faith, competing for the minds and loyalties of mankind. Perhaps the most challenging of all these "isms" to the church is secularism.

What is secularism? Where are its roots and to what extent has secularism penetrated contemporary society? How did Western culture emerge from a sacral to a secular way of life? To what degree has secularism seeped into the church? How can the church resist the corroding acids of secularism and relate itself in freedom to a secular society?

A. SECULARIZATION OF SOCIETY

The term "secularism" has an interesting pedigree. It is derived from the Latin word *saeculum*, meaning "of or belonging to an age or generation." Taken directly from the Latin, the term "secular" means "lasting" or "occurring over a long indefinite period of time" and is used in scientific application to processes or phenomena that continue through the ages as, for example, "the secular cooling of the earth."

In the medieval period, the term "secular" was used, first, to denote that which belongs to this world, the nonspiritual. It was used to distinguish the "regular" or monastic clergy from the parish priests, the "seculars" who lived in the world. Secondly, the term was used to refer to the temporal as opposed to the spiritual or ecclesiastical. Hence, property transferred from religious to temporal hands was said to be "secularized." Secular education, for example, was held to be a system in which there is no religious teaching and over which the church has no control.[1] In some circles today, the word "secular" has taken on a pejorative connotation, meaning that which is opposed to or the enemy of the church. And secularism is seen as a secular faith that threatens the Christian faith.

1. Some Definitions of Secularism and Secularization

Secularism is one of those terms which requires at least an operational definition in order to avoid semantical sand traps. It is defined as "that characteristic of our world according to which life is organized apart from God, as though God did not exist."[2] Secularism is also defined as "the absence of the religious, transcendent, or ultimate dimension or reference in all the facets of life, and the consequent derivation of all standards and goals solely from the natural and social environments in which men live."[3] Again, it is defined as "our failure to let God be God in our lives. Its nature is neither to affirm nor to deny religious faith, but to live indifferently to it."[4] Secularism is "the name for an ideology, a new closed world-view which functions very much like a new religion."[5] In short, it is "the ordering and conducting of life as if God did not exist."[6]

From the above definitions we derive three basic elements that characterize secularism. First, in secularism there is no transcendent factor. God is ruled out. Second, ethical standards are derived from one's environment or culture. Third, secularism is a closed world view that in actuality becomes another religion, a secular faith.

This brings us to the term "secularization," which must be distinguished from secularism. The former is the process of man's turning away from transcendent religion toward a world view limiting itself to life on the human plane. Charles West defines this process as "the withdrawal of areas of life and thought from religious—and finally also from metaphysical—control, and the attempt to understand and live in these areas in the terms of which they alone offer."[7] The key, then, to the understanding of the distinction between secularism and secularization is that of *process:* man's turning away from transcendence, other worlds, to this world where religion is no longer relevant for his existence.

Secularization proceeds in the direction of a secular culture or society. D. L. Munby describes a secular society as one that refuses to commit itself as a whole to any particular view of nature, as heterogeneous, as tolerant, without official images, and one in which problems can be solved by facing the facts.[8]

Secular society receives vivid description by Cox in what he calls the "secular city."[9] As a result of the secularization process, he thinks that man has moved from a tribal to a town culture, and is now evolving into "technopolis," a new species of human community. *Techno* symbolizes the technical basis on which the secular city rests, while *polis* represents its social and cultural institutions.

The secular city's social *shape* is derived from two images: the switchboard (the key to communications in the city, the linking of human beings together), and the cloverleaf (the image of mobility). These symbols illustrate, then, two basic characteristics of the city—anonymity and mobility. Rather than decrying these as destructive of persons, Cox emphasizes their positive side by demonstrating that both contribute to the sustenance of life in the city.[10]

The *style* of the secular city refers "to the way a society . . . organizes the values and meanings by which it lives."[11] Pragmatism and profanity are two motifs that characterize the secular city's style, the former denoting man's concern with things that work for him and the latter with his wholly terrestrial existence. Technopolitan man, in his pragmatism and profanity, is to be affirmed by the church; for the gospel, declares Cox, "is not a call to man to abandon his interest in the problems of this world, but an invitation to accept the full weight of this world's problems as the gift of its Maker; . . . a call to be a man of this technical age, with all that means, seeking to make it a human habitation for all who live within it."[12]

2. The Dynamics of Secularization

The secularization process in the Western world has its dynamics in both Biblical and non-Biblical sources. Secularization first arose in Western culture as a result of the impact of Biblical faith on history.[13] The Biblical view of Creation not only separates God from nature but also distinguishes man from nature, emancipating him from superstition and the gods of nature. This is what Cox calls "the disenchantment of nature."[14] In God's act of creation, the world is depopulated of those spirits which were once thought to control man and his destiny. Hence, there are no spirits active in the physical world that can bless or punish humanity. Ordering and keeping the world is transferred from the hands of demons and gods to the hands of men. In a creation purged of demons and stripped of its idolatries, man can live by faith in the one true God and in creative freedom toward the world.

Biblical faith also secularizes politics. In primitive tribal society as well as in more enlightened cultures, there is an identification of the religious and political orders in which the ruler is believed to be divine and to rule by divine sanction. Any political change depends upon the desacralization of politics. Cox thinks that God's action in the exodus event, a historical event, was an action against a divine ruler under the god Re and that it opened up the possibility of political and social change. Hence, the exodus, which delivered the Jews from Egypt, symbolizes the deliverance of man from the sacral-political order into historical and political change. From the exodus event to the present day, this desacralizing impact has been felt in the realm of politics in such events as the struggle of the popes with political rulers and the separation of church and state in America.[15]

Biblical faith secularizes the law. God's prohibition against all idolatry and the replication of himself in the form of images demotes all other gods and relativizes all human values that they represent. For primitive people, their gods and value systems are viewed as one and the same. Hence, to devalue their gods is to also downgrade and to make relative the values that they require.

Within the Bible itself, laws are modified and even abrogated from time to time as the situation demands. Laws given at the time of the exodus were decried by the eighth-century prophets. Jesus radically modified the laws pertaining to the Jewish Sabbath and gave a deeper meaning to the Ten Commandments.

Nature, politics, and the law have felt the desacralizing impact of the Judeo-Christian faith. Man, who has been called into existence by God, has also been called to existence-in-responsibility, to have dominion over the world, to "till it and keep it" free from the control of false gods and idolatrous practices.

The process of secularization also has non-Biblical sources.[16] It was given impetus by the scientific discoveries of such men as Galileo, Newton, Descartes, and Darwin, along with the philosophies of men like Machiavelli, Hobbes, Comte, and Marx. Such developments as industrialization, urbanization, and technology have also paved the way for a secularized society in the world today.

Secularization moves toward secularism, a system of values without any reference to transcendence. As an ideology and system of ethics, secularism found expression about 1846 in the thought of George Jacob Holyoake of England. Among the basic postulates of Holyoake's system are the right to freedom of thought, the right to difference of opinion upon all subjects of thought, the right to assert differences of opinion, and the right to discuss and to debate vital questions such as moral obligation, the existence of God, and immortality.[17] Contemporary secularism, as an ideology, is much more complex with an absolute this-wordly posture in which man derives his values completely divorced from spiritual reality.

3. The Degree of Secularization

Both Western man and his culture have become highly secularized. The extent of secularization is difficult to establish, for it varies with different countries. Dr. Steven Mackie, reporting the opinion of delegates to the "Life and Mission of the Church" conference of the World Council of Churches meeting at Gratz, January, 1963, declares that Britain, most European countries, and Russia are almost fully secularized, particularly with reference to their universities, natural and social sciences, and welfare efforts.[18]

During the first half of this century, secularism has had a serious effect on the churches in Britain and Europe. In 1957, this writer was informed by Mr. Sorensen, M.P., that only 5 percent of the British people attend church. His explanation for nonattendance at church was that churches had become irrelevant, that science and labor unions met the needs of the people.

There are indications that in the United States secularization is rapidly reaching an advanced stage. American universities are becoming more and more oriented toward secularity. Originally founded for religious purposes, colleges such as Harvard, Brown, Princeton, Yale, and others have been and are being weaned away from church control and church doctrine.

Attempts of the churches to maintain influence over colleges and universities have met with little success. Few "Christian colleges" have any real religious orientation despite the religious mottoes inscribed on their seals. Work through local churches in college communities with specialized ministries is largely bankrupt. Even the churches' efforts to follow students into colleges by way of denominational student organizations have not been very effective. This approach siphons off a few students from the mainstream of university life into denominational cocoons. Hence, there is little real penetration of the intellectual and moral life of the campus by these religious groups.

The churches of America betray the marks of secularity. Captives of their culture, some churches reflect a faith against God rather than for him. Big-business methods with too much emphasis upon "success" in terms of big budgets and big programs for their own enhancement characterize many contemporary congregations. Churches and the success cult are becoming closely intertwined. One American minister offers the following formula for financial success: "Prayerize," "Picturize," and "Actualize."[19]

William H. Whyte, Jr., reports that in a suburban section of Chicago a survey was made as to what influenced people there in choosing a church. In order of importance, the following factors were listed: (a) the minister, (b) the Sunday school, (c) the location, (d) the denomination, and (e) the music.[20] While these factors may not apply in every community, one suspects that they widely prevail in suburbia. Apparently people are looking for a comfortable, convenient, and cozy church. There is a noticeable absence of emphasis upon theology in depth and the spiritual and moral function of the Holy Spirit in contemporary churches. An executive of a large corporation told a group of laymen that at the church which he attended, the Holy Spirit could walk right out the back door and nobody would miss him!

In too many instances the Christian faith has devolved into civic religiosity, a religion of the masses, the cult of the American way of life. This is a radical religiosity, a synthesis of patriotism, capitalism, tolerance, and affluency. God is conceived as a "Good Guy" and "fun to know," a God to be manipulated to satisfy the hunger for peace and security.

In spite of the fact that church attendance is at an all-time high, increasingly fewer and fewer Americans take Biblical Christianity seriously and accept its ethical teachings as guidelines for daily living. Interviewers for the American Institute of Public Opinion asked adult Americans who considered religion to be something "very important" in their lives, "Would you say your religious beliefs have any effect on your ideas of politics and business?" Fifty-four percent said no,[21] in spite of the fact that practically all polls show that from 97 to 98 percent of Americans believe in God. T.S. Eliot may be right when he says that religion has become a sort of "social tonic that can be used in times of national emergency in order to extract a further degree of moral effort from the people."[22]

The church is afloat on a sea of secularism that is seeping into its hull. As Karl Heim vividly puts it: "Amid this rising flood of secularism there floats the ark of the Church. The Church is like a ship on whose deck festivities are still kept up and glorious music is heard, while deep below the water-line a leak has been sprung and masses of water are pouring in, so that the vessel is settling hourly lower though the pumps are manned day and night."[23]

Thus, Western culture and its churches are being gradually enfolded in the covers of a secular society. There is no way to measure accurately the degree to which man and his institutions have become secularized. Some indication may be seen in Pitirim Sorokin's observation that in the twelfth and thirteenth centuries, 97 percent of the subjects of the fine arts were devoted to religious motifs against 3 percent depicting secular life. Today the ratio is almost exactly the opposite.[24]

B. THE SERVANT CHURCH

To meet the challenge of secular society is the task of theology today. A growing number of theologians are responding to the secular situation.

Enlarging upon Bonhoeffer's brief statements about "religionless Christianity," some theologians are attempting to develop a theology of true secularity.[25] In this study the focus will be upon the problem of Christology and the nature of the church in a secular theology.

1. The New Christology

A theology of true secularity requires a shift away from traditional interpretations of Jesus. The theologians of secularity, taking their cue from Bonhoeffer, see Jesus as "the man for others" to be followed in his humiliation and imitated in terms of love for neighbor and striving for justice in the world. The *locus classicus* of this new Christology is Phil. 2:5-11. Here Christ is pictured as emptying himself and as taking on human and servant form. In this event, Christ identified himself with man in the flesh and made known his Lordship by becoming servant of all. Christ's coming into the world in the form of man was a secular event. God "secularizes" himself in this man Jesus and whoever finds "in this man his own humanity will discover himself also."[26]

God comes in Jesus to "desacralize" religion and to break down the barriers between the sacred and the secular. Hence, Jesus spent much of his time attacking institutions through which man had transformed the true faith into an organized religion.[27]

In Jesus Christ, according to Bonhoeffer, the world has been reconciled to God and there are no longer two realms, the sacred and the profane. He declares: "Sharing in Christ we stand at once both in the reality of God and the reality of the world. The reality of Christ comprises the reality of the world within itself. The world has no reality of its own, independently of the revelation of God in Christ. . . . There are, therefore, not two spheres, but only the one sphere of the realization of Christ, in which the reality of God and the reality of the world are united."[28]

Since the world is reconciled to God in Christ, the church should seek no radical separation for itself from the world. Rather, as Jesus was the man for others, the church must be for others in the world. Bonhoeffer does modify his radical position by noting that ultimately—that is, eschatologically—the distinction between church and world disappears, but penultimately, the distinction remains. However, the church must bear evidence that it lives in the light of the *eschaton* in which it hopes.[29]

2. The Servanthood of the Church

The new Christology has implications for the nature and form of the church. Even as Jesus took the form of man and a servant, even so the church must take the form of men and minister in servant form. This involves self-emptying, service, and solidarity with people.[30] Just as Christ exists for others, the church is to exist not for itself but for others. This does not mean that the church lives in coexistence with the world, but in *proexistence* for the world.[31]

Hence, the church must take the form of Christ in the world. "The task therefore of the Church," says John A. T. Robinson, "is to *be* this Son of Man on earth, allowing its imperfect incarnation to be judged constantly by *the* Incarnation."[32] In short, the servant ministry of the church finds its model in the life and ministry of Jesus, who "came not to be served but to serve, and to give his life as a ransom for many" (Matt. 20:28).

When the church takes "kenotic form," it empties itself so that it can take the shape in which it can minister most effectively to the world. To be the servant church, to be proexistent, it must find new forms of Christian community for a new age. This means that in order to minister within the diverse communities in the world, the church must break out of old institutional molds. Much emphasis is placed upon the renewal of the church. But the institutional structures have become so rigid as to be impervious to renewal. Radical new forms that the church must assume today demand reformation. Every sacrosanct structure that stands in the way of these new shapes of the church must be axed.

Richard Shaull's employment of the figure of the Jewish Dispersion to describe the life of Christians in the modern world is a fruitful one.[33] In our highly mobile culture, millions of people (thirty-six million in the U.S. in 1965) move from old to new residences, transplanted in the dispersion. City churches often become "pigeon-loft congregations, where people come and fly off again, and who knows where?"[34] They are "here today and gone tomorrow" and often lost to the church in the anonymity of urbanism. To minister more adequately to these people and to secular man, the church must take the form of Christ in community organizations, political associations, the family, and numerous other areas of society.

While the essence of the church does not change, it must take on new forms to establish communication and community in the changing situation. As Dietrich Bonhoeffer declares, the church is "Christ existing as community."[35] Indeed, his form is community, the form that the church, his body, is to take in the secular community.

What are the authentic forms or new shapes that the servant church can take in secular society? Among the new forms of the church expressing themselves today are: lay movements, house churches, movable chapels, coffeehouses, and groups demonstrating for racial and economic justice.[36] These approaches to secular culture are still in the experimental stage. No doubt numerous other new forms of the church will appear as it seeks to take the form of Christ where men live, work, and play.

In America, new strategies are being developed to make the servant church relevant in urban society. Gibson Winter believes that the laymen who are involved "in the processes of society and develop theological sensitivity form the only possible Church in mass society."[37] Instead of thrusting people into the world for ministry, institutional churches tend to draw people into a program, keep them busy in a maze of organizations, and divert their attention away from public responsibility. Winter insists that churches in suburban captivity, concerned with the preservation of private virtues, must extend their ministry to the whole metropolis.[38]

Since the issues in the secular metropolis are political, theology must take on a political mode. Paul Lehmann stresses the view that what God is doing in the world is politics, which means making and keeping human life human.[39] Politics describes man's role in response to God, reflecting and analyzing what it takes to make and keep human life human in the world. Similarly, Harvey Cox thinks the task of theology today is to point the church to the place where God the politician is acting and to join him as co-workers.[40] Hence, theology assumes a political mode and politics is substituted for metaphysics as the terminology of theology. Thus, one way "to speak of God in a secular fashion" (to use Bonhoeffer's phrase) is to place ourselves where the restoring and reconciling activity of God is taking place, where the proper relationship between human beings is occurring. The church is to be "God's avant garde" in this sort of ministry.[41]

The new theology of secularity, therefore, plays down the notion of the church as an institution. Rather, the servant church is a fellowship of "the people of God." Such a view of the church liberates its members for freedom and engagement in the world where God is at work redeeming and reconciling mankind. The work of God in the world, where Christ is present, is likened to a "floating crap game" and the church is a confirmed gambler whose "major compulsion upon arising each day is to know where the action is" so he can run there and "dig it."[42] The task of the church, therefore, is to see where God in Christ is acting in the social order and to take this shape or form.

The congregation in mission, therefore, must think politically as to its role in the world, because God is active in politics in the sense of making human life human. As George Webber notes, "The church, in sharing in God's politics, is called to discern what God is doing, to share in his task, and finally to point to what God is doing."[43] To discern what God is doing in the world, the congregation must "listen, converse, and learn to love the world around its doors."[44]

In the new theology of secularity, evangelism is politics. Proponents of this view draw upon Philippe Maury, who speaks of political action as "the language of evangelism."[45] The main task of the lay political "evangelists" is to infiltrate the power structures of the community where decisions are being made that shape it and there bear their witness with the view to making and keeping human life human. Here there is no thought of making man into a *homo religiosus*, but that of restoring him to normal human manhood in a more just society. After all, it is reasoned, Christians are ultimately judged on the basis of their ministry to human need, a service to persons they will not even remember. Yet they will be ministering to Christ *incognito* (the parable of the sheep and the goats, Matt. 25:31–46).[46]

New forms of the church require a new image of the clergy, along with a committed and intelligent laity. The traditional view of the clergyman is that of the laymen helping him to do his work. This defines the role of the laymen as aids to the pastor in his ministry. In contrast, the New Testament teaches that every Christian is called to be a minister. It is the task of the pastor, then, to "equip" the laity for "the work of ministry" (Eph. 4:12). This is a complete reversal of their roles in contemporary churches. Yet, it is the function of the clergy to assist the laity to be the church. The call of the laity is to be "politicians" in the world, while the clergy in the church equip them for this ministry.[47]

A problem is raised as to how the church can prepare a laity theologically aware and socially sensitive. At present, theological training is largely confined to seminaries for the training of professional church-related personnel. Here the clergyman is trained as a "theological specialist" who often becomes merely a personal counselor and an administrative expert. Winter claims that the clergyman is needed primarily as a theological resource man for the prophetic fellowship or lay servanthood.[48] Actual training of the servanthood of the laity for witness in the world would not necessarily take place in institutional churches, but in "evangelical centers" and "academies." Perhaps Winter feels that these centers should not be church-related, because the institutional church is alienated from the dynamic, creative areas of society.

The question appropriately arises as to what is the place of prayer and worship in "religionless Christianity" or "worldly holiness." Robinson answers that worship is to make us more sensitive to the secular world, to "deepen our response to the world and to other people, . . . to purify and correct our lives in the light of Christ's love; and in him to find the grace and power to be the reconciled and reconciling community."[49] Prayer becomes an active engagement in self-giving service to others rather than withdrawal for meditation in the traditional sense.[50] The usual disciplined prayer life may be good for those who are "religious," but for "man come of age" there is freedom in Christ that allows him to discover for himself what prayer is and what form it takes, even if this is a "nonreligious" form.[51] Hence, the life of worship and prayer is "nonreligious," transcending the false dichotomy between the sacred and the secular.

C. CRITICAL EVALUATION AND THE CONTINUING SEARCH

Theologians of secularity have made some significant contributions toward more realistic approaches of the church vis-à-vis secular society. At the same time, their views betray certain weaknesses that must be noted. This final statement attempts to specify both the strengths and the shortcomings of the proponents of "religionless Christianity" for secular society.

1. Sensitivity to the Contribution of Secularism

For one thing, the men cited in this study have called attention to the significance of secularism for the church. Christians, generally, denounce secularism as wholly evil and destructive to the church. Recently, however, a number of Christian thinkers have been noting the beneficial effects of secularism. Instead of viewing secularism as a foe, they argue that the church should recognize in it a friend. Thus, theologian Langdon Gilkey lists the values of secularism to the church in terms of having learned: (a) "a respect for science and the tentativeness of all truth"; (b) "an active distaste for the concrete evils of this life and a concern to eradicate them"; (c) "a tolerance of opposing communions and faiths"; (d) "an acceptance of the joys and pleasures as well as the crises and sorrows of this life"; and (e) "a rejection of the legalism and creedalism that were demonic elements in its own past."[52] He draws the conclusion that secularism has been a more faithful prophetic critic of the church than the church has been of the world.[53]

D. L. Munby, of Oxford, holds with Dietrich Bonhoeffer that a secular society enlarges the area of men's choices and calls men to a greater maturity.[54] Harvey Cox has written in praise of the secularization of the modern city and its liberties, reminding us that its new freedom requires new maturity and a new measure of responsibility. Gilkey reminds us that if a better gospel is preached by the church and its members live more creatively now than in the earlier dogmatic, moralistic, intolerant days, it is partly due to the criticism of the secular world.[55]

Edwin E. Aubrey declares that instead of the churches treating secular organizations with contempt, they should recognize them as allies in the struggle for righteousness, for they have produced many spiritual values.[56] Certainly the Christian community has been helped by such forces as the Red Cross, the National Polio Foundation, the P.T.A., welfare agencies, Boy Scouts and Girl Scouts, and similar organizations. These agencies can be an asset to the churches if members will work through them to effect better communities and a more wholesome way of life.

Secularization has helped to free us from the intolerance, bigotry, and ignorance foisted upon man by ecclesiastical forces, and we can be grateful that the process is still going on in Protestantism and to some degree in Catholicism.

2. Dangerous Trends in Secular Theology

But this sort of emphasis on the secularization of the Christian faith has its dangers. It must be remembered that secularization tends toward secularism, a closed world view, which is another religion. Secular or "religionless Christianity" may simply articulate the values of secular culture, the ideological, moralistic, bourgeois standards of the American middle class. There is the ever-present process of resacralization in a secularized society that may result in the resacralization of the church itself in terms of the substitution of religious structures and authorities for the gospel of Christ. Where there is no clear distinction between the sacred and the secular, the former becomes a curious mixture in which secular man is provided a thin cloak of religious respectability to cover his self-centered-ness and self-deification.

There is a tendency in the theologians of secularity to make Christianity compatible with secular culture rather than bringing it to terms with Christianity.[57] Hence, there is the possibility of the church's losing itself in the world and becoming just another social institution. Christianity is to transform culture, not to be conformed to it.

In the radical theology of secularity there is a sacrifice of transcendence. The disciples of Bonhoeffer go beyond his view of the ultimate and penultimate realities by ignoring the dialectical tension between the two. Actually in Bonhoeffer, the penultimate has no value in itself.[58] There is such a shift of emphasis in the theology of secularity as to make the ultimate for all practical purposes irrelevant.

The Christian faith is both transcendent and immanent, both radically otherworldly and this-worldly. The authentic secularity of the church is that of living under the sovereignty of the cosmic Christ. He who is Lord of the individual is also Lord of secular society. He is at work outside as well as inside the church.

Moreover, as G. S. Wilmore declares: "The Lordship of Christ over the secular does not mean that the church is at peace with the world."[59] Authentic Christian secularism is characterized by a sober this-worldliness, a shaking off of the illusions of culture, a sharing of a certain empiricism about reality and existence, possessing a basic humanistic passion for justice, truth, and freedom in common with secularists on behalf of a deeper secularity. The kind of secularism that encourages the "rationalization and routinization" of the *status quo* is simply not worldly enough.[60]

The Christology of the theologians of secularity is open to criticism. Overly stressing Jesus as "the man for others" may result in his reduction to the status of mere man. Denial of

Jesus' virgin birth and of the reality of the resurrection tends to deny that God in Christ entered into the secular. With reference to the virgin birth of Jesus and the "biological details," Robinson declares: "Nothing for me depends on them."[61] For Robinson, the resurrection is not something that happened to Jesus, but an overwhelming experience to his disciples. As for Jesus' literal resurrection or the appearance of an "astral body," Robinson considers this all quite secondary.[62] Robinson appears to reject the supernaturalistic and naturalistic realities in connection with the coming of Christ into the world. He categorically states that Jesus is not God, though he does bring God completely in himself.[63]

All the theologians of secularity, of course, are not in agreement with all the elements of Robinson's Christology. However, they do stress Jesus as "the man for others" to the neglect of the other dimensions of his nature. In his book *The Secular City*, Cox gives little attention to Christ and makes only two references to the cross. In general, secular theologians stress the humanity of Jesus to the neglect of his unique, divine nature. Hence, the man Jesus is portrayed as the highest model of freedom, love, and justice. It is doubtful that secular man responds any more readily to this sort of Christ than to the traditional view of him as the God-man.

Finally, in the thought of the theologians of secularity, there is a tendency to absolutize Jesus "the man for others." This view of him is abstracted from the totality of New Testament Christology and becomes *the* Christological reality. Here, Bonhoeffer serves as a corrective of his own disciples. He says:

In Jesus Christ we have faith in the incarnate, crucified and risen God. In the incarnation we learn of the love of God for His creation; in the crucifixion we learn of the judgement of God upon all flesh; and in the resurrection we learn of God's will for a new world. There could be no greater error than to tear these three elements apart; for each of them comprises the whole. It is quite wrong to establish a separate theology of the incarnation, a theology of the cross, or a theology of the resurrection, each in opposition to the others, by a misconceived absolutization of one of these parts; it is equally wrong to apply the same procedure to a consideration of the Christian life. A Christian ethic constructed solely on the basis of the incarnation would lead directly to the compromise solution. An ethic which was based solely on the cross or the resurrection of Jesus would fall victim to radicalism and enthusiasm. Only in the unity is the conflict resolved.[64]

Emphasis upon the servanthood of the church through the laity is the forte of the advocates of "religionless Christianity." To meet the challenge of secular society, the church must become engaged in the world, but not immersed in it. Its voice must be heard and its influence felt where decisions are being made that can make human life more human. But in so doing, the church must not lose itself in the world by becoming captive to worldly ways and values.

To stress new forms of the church, as do the theologians of secularity, at the expense of the institutional church is to ignore the authentic ministry being performed in them. There is still much good being done through the old structures. Another weakness in the new approach to secularity by the servant church advocates is that of playing down the dialectic between transcendence and relevance in the church's relation to the world. The church was established by God's act in Christ who sustains it by his grace. Without this transcendent dimension held in relevance to the secular world, the church becomes a mere uplift club with a cultural piety. It should be added that evangelism is more than politics, because it aims at both the regeneration of the individual and the transformation of society. True evangelism seeks to bring all men and institutions under the Lordship of Christ. Finally, worship involves more than merely sensitizing us to the secular, and prayer is more than simply being actively engaged in self-giving service to others. Like Kant, the theologians of secularity tend to completely ethicize worship and prayer. In both worship and prayer there are the dimensions of contemplation, withdrawal, and meditation. If Jesus himself felt the need to withdraw and pray in the "traditional" sense (Luke 22:41), should not his disciples? Jesus taught them to do so. (Matt. 6:6.)

3. Calling and Secular Culture

One concluding statement appears to be in order. Theologians of secularity tend to neglect the most effective doctrine for Christian confrontation with the world. This is the Christian doctrine of calling or vocation in both its theological and ethical dimensions.[65] Church historian James H. Nichols has rightly noted that the Protestant Reformation concept of vocations "became the means of the greatest penetration of Christianity into culture which the history of the faith has seen."[66] This came about, not by clerical intervention in political, economic, and social life, but by Protestant "monks-in-the-world." A recovery of the Christian doctrine of calling, as the integrating symbol of the Christian's life and function, would make it possible for the church, through the laity, to penetrate more effectively our secular society with the transforming power of the gospel of the living Christ.

The problem today is not the church in the world, but the world in the church. Jesus prayed, not that Christians should be taken out of the world, but that the Father would keep them from the evil one (John 17:15). The church, therefore, is saved in the world, from the world, and for the world. The Christian is summoned to God for redemption and sent into the world to participate in his eternal purpose of uniting all things in Christ by a ministry of reconciliation. When the Christian accepts the call to vocation, he has nowhere to stand except in and with the secular.

V. THE NEW DIMENSIONS OF WAR:
"THINKING ABOUT THE UNTHINKABLE"

WAR is one of those persistent evils which has plagued man from the beginning of his history. Arnold Toynbee, the English historian, declares that today war "is the crucial question on which the destiny of our civilization hangs."[1] Emil Brunner, the late Swiss theologian, speaking of war, says: "We are here confronted by one of the most controversial ethical problems of the present day."[2] New weapons of mass destruction—nuclear, chemical, bacteriological, and radiological—have heightened the moral factors involved in warfare. Now we face the possibility of a global war in which there may be a thermonuclear annihilation of the human race or "totalicide." This situation prompted the late President Kennedy to assert: "Mankind must put an end to war or war will put an end to mankind."

The aim of this chapter is to look briefly at war in historical perspective, to describe the nature of nuclear warfare along with the moral issues involved, and to suggest ways in which the church can make a contribution to peace.

A. WARS PAST

Amos, the Hebrew prophet, describes war as a cruel harvest of iron, of human blood and human lives (Amos 1:3). General Sherman is quoted as saying: "War is hell." Some sociologists see war as an armed conflict "between organized bodies of people, regarding themselves as politically sovereign and ethically entitled to assert by force their rights, which they claim to be blocked or invaded by their armed opponents."[3] No matter how one defines war, it is a terrible and horrifying evil.

The frequency of war is astounding. From 500 B.C. to A.D. 1924 there have been 967 major interstate wars in the history of Greece, Rome, Austria, Germany, England, France, the Netherlands, Spain, Italy, Russia, Poland, and Lithuania. Such wars have occurred on an average of one every two and one half years. Periods of peace as long as a quarter of a century have been exceedingly rare.[4]

In the United States, no generation has been free from war. The United States has engaged in nine major conflicts, an average of one every twenty-five years, since 1776. The present war in Vietnam may last for years, while other so-called wars of national liberation may break out in Southeast Asia and in Latin America.

In this century, wars have become global in magnitude. Prior to 1914, our fathers were screened from the threat of total warfare by two oceans. But with the development of rockets that carry nuclear warheads, and now orbital rocketry, all natural barriers to world conflict have been removed. Today, no place on earth is invulnerable to attack. In the words of the Negro spiritual, there is literally "no hiding place."

The cost of war in terms of human life and money increases with each occurrence. In World War I, approximately 8,000,-000 soldiers lost their lives and 21,000,000 were wounded. In World War II approximately 19,500,000 military men were killed along with 13,000,000 civilians. The U.S. lost almost 1,000,000 men. More than 23,000 lost their lives in the Korean conflict, not to mention the deaths among our allies and the hundreds of thousands of enemy and civilians killed.

In terms of money, war is an expensive business. It has been estimated that in Caesar's day the cost of killing a man in battle was 75 cents. In Napoleon's time the cost had increased to $3,000; by the time of the Civil War, it had increased to

$5,000; by the end of World War I, to $21,000; and in World War II the United States paid the equivalent of $50,000 per capita for its dead enemies.[5] It is estimated that today it costs the United States $375,000 to kill one Viet Cong.[6]

According to the Defense Department, World War I cost the United States 25 billion dollars; World War II, more than 323 billion dollars; and the Korean conflict, 20 billion. In 1966 alone, the war in Vietnam cost us roughly 20 billion dollars. More than 60 percent of our total national budget is now allocated for defense and military purposes.

B. THE NEW DIMENSIONS OF WAR

There is simply no parallel between wars past and the kind of destruction that would result in a nuclear war. The nature and effects of such a cataclysm that would be caused by an all-out nuclear war is unthinkable; and we are most reluctant to "think about the unthinkable."[7]

The atom bomb that destroyed Hiroshima, snuffed out 100,000 lives, and destroyed every house within a radius of two miles was the first primitive firecracker of the Atomic Age. Today we possess bombs with megatonic and multimegatonic force. One twenty-megaton H-bomb delivers more explosive power than all the weapons used in all the wars of history.[8]

The terrifying dimensions of the destructive potential of nuclear weapons have been dramatically described by the experts. David Inglis, senior physicist at Argonne National Laboratory in Illinois, holds that on a clear day, a ten-megaton bomb (one of the smaller megaton family), exploded in the atmosphere thirty miles above the earth, could set fire to combustibles over an area of 5,000 square miles. A surface burst from this same bomb would produce a crater about 250 feet deep and a half mile wide. The zone of complete destruction would be about three miles in diameter. Severe blasts would extend to about nine miles from the center of the explosion, and moderate damage would extend out to twelve miles. Also, attendant effects would be felt, such as "fire storms" of hurricane velocities. Radioactive products would be scattered all over the countryside as "fallout."[9] One can imagine what would happen to a city like New York after being hit by one of these monsters.

It has been estimated that a fifteen-hundred-megaton bomb attack on 224 centers in the United States would result in the death or injury of one third of the population. Nearly 25 million deaths could be expected on the first day and an additional 25 million persons would be fatally injured. An additional 20 million would be injured, but not fatally.[10]

The swiftness of delivery of the H-bomb is incredible and fantastic. A ballistic missile can carry one of these bombs from Moscow to Washington in about thirty minutes. At the most, we would have fifteen minutes warning of an approaching missile. An all-out nuclear war would probably be over in from three to thirty days.

Another frightening aspect is that a nuclear war could be triggered accidentally. No instrument is perfect and man is not completely free from error of judgment. Misinterpretation of radar data and administrative accidents are within the realm of possibility.

Stockpiling of nuclear weapons continues apace to the point of "overkill capacity." The United States now possesses over 2,500 megatons of explosive power, more than enough to destroy the Soviet Union. The Soviets have already exploded a fifty-megaton bomb. According to Victor Karpov, first secretary of the Soviet Embassy in Washington, the Soviets have produced the gigaton bomb with the potential of one thousand megatons. Now comes the report that the Soviets possess an orbital nuclear missile capable of carrying a one-hundred-megaton warhead which they claim could orbit the earth and strike America from any direction, evading our warning system. An all-out use of such weapons would mean the destruction of civilization. Professor Albert Einstein was probably right when he declared that he did not know what kind of weapons would be used in the next war, but in the subsequent war, it would be stone clubs.

Such are the terrifying prospects of a nuclear catastrophe. The use of such weapons of mass destruction may well be the most important moral decision ever to confront the Christian conscience. What should be the Christian's stance vis-à-vis nuclear warfare? There is no easy answer.

C. CHRISTIAN ATTITUDES TOWARD WAR

Historical perspective of the various postures of the church toward war may provide some guidelines for the contemporary Christian. Roland Bainton has written a helpful book on Christian attitudes toward war and peace throughout the history of the church.[11] Here he shows that three distinctive stances have been expressed by Christians toward participation in war. These are pacifism, the just war, and the holy crusade.

1. The Pacifist Position

The early church was prevailingly pacifist in its view toward engagement in war. C. J. Cadoux quotes from many church fathers—Justin Martyr, Origen, Clement of Alexandria, Tertullian, Cyprian, and others—to prove that the church prior to A.D. 313 was opposed to Christian participation in battle.[12]

All through the centuries there have been historic minorities of Christian pacifists such as the Anabaptists, the Mennonites, and the Quakers. Two major types of pacifists appear among Christians—legalistic and redemptive. Legalists take literally such Scripture texts as Ex. 20:13; Matt. 5:39; and Matt. 26:52. They give no consideration to the social consequences of their actions and do not expect to influence a majority of unregenerate humanity. Jehovah's Witnesses espouse this view, contending that Christians will always be "sheep among wolves."

Redemptive pacifists hold that just as Jesus' sufferings were redemptive, so, in the long run, nonviolent resistance to tyranny will be effective. Exponents of this position take Christ and the early church as norms of conduct regarding war.[13] They find a New Testament basis for redemptive pacifism. The primacy of love is emphasized. For them, *agapē* is the very nature of God and the central ethical imperative of the Christian's conduct. Such love is more than goodwill or kindness; it is self-giving for the good of others; it is both uncalculating (Matt. 5:10) and all-inclusive of friend and foe (Matt. 5:38 ff.). Divine retributive justice is God's business. Hence, war is ruled out.

Another principle of the redemptive pacifist is that of overcoming evil with good. Paul is taken seriously when he says: "'If your enemy is hungry, feed him; if he is thirsty, give him drink; for by so doing you will heap burning coals upon his head.' Do not be overcome by evil but overcome evil with good" (Rom. 12:20–21). Jesus himself set the example for the Christian. When Jesus was being crucified, he did not strike back; and while on the cross, he prayed to the Father to forgive those who were putting him to death.

A final principle common to all redemptive pacifists is the means-end relation. Good ends do not justify bad means. Paul is cited again when he declares: "And why not do evil that good may come?—as some people slanderously charge us with saying" (Rom. 3:8). Here Paul is accused of holding the view that the Christian may do evil that good may come of it. He responds by noting that those whose reason leads to such a conclusion deserve the condemnation that falls upon them.

With the advent of nuclear weapons and their possible use, all pacifists and some nonpacifists in principle declare that they are "nuclear pacifists." Roland Bainton is adamantly opposed to nuclear welfare. While he personally embraces pacifism, it is not absolute but relative pacifism. This is borne out in his statement: "If peace is preserved it will be through the efforts not of pacifists, but of peace-minded nonpacifists, who do not renounce war absolutely, but who oppose war in our time on grounds of the humanitarian and the pragmatic."[14] Thus, he has a double standard for church and state, the latter based on natural law, the former on the gospel ethic. From natural law, he derives the principles of rationality and universality, a utilitarian ethic that dictates to men and nations that they should act for the universal good rather than for self-interest.

Bainton makes the interesting observation that man responds more readily to an ideal than to a material goal.[15] He thus suggests that unilateral disarmament and nonviolence "might revolutionize the world's behavior" in the nuclear crisis. He raises the question as to what would happen if our nation were to disarm unilaterally. It might have an amazing effect. But no proof of this can be offered, because no nation has ever tried it. He concludes with, "But if not," words spoken by the three Jewish youths who were commanded by Nebuchadnezzar to worship a golden image or be cast into the fiery furnace (Dan. 3:1–18). "But if not" we should be prepared to suffer the grim prospects and disadvantages that might come as a result of unilateral disarmament. The prospects are grim, he admits, but so is the threat of annihilation. Besides, if we were subjected to communism, what would emerge after a century is difficult to see. But the spirit of man is resurgent, and more than once in history "the descendants of conquerors have looked upon themselves as spiritually the sons of the conquered."[16]

A statement issued by pacifists, including George Buttrick, formerly preacher to Harvard University, states that the conqueror may impose mental and physical suffering on the conquered, but an ordeal of this sort "could not be as acute and meaningless a form of suffering as that bound to occur in an eruption of atomic warfare."[17]

Concrete proposals for practical implementation of the principles of reconciliation, sacrifice, and atonement are made by Buttrick and his colleagues in seven points: (a) immediate negotiation for *multilateral* disarmament; (b) refusal of Christians to sanction the use or possession of nuclear or other mass destruction weapons; (c) universal withdrawal from the arms race in the event multilateral disarmament cannot be achieved; (d) negotiation for disengagement of troops from various areas and neutralization of these areas; (e) extrication from military alliances with imperialist and reactionary regimes; (f) serious study of the possibilities of nonviolent resistance; and (g) rejection of the notion widely held that Christian

values can be defended, and our Lord and his teaching somehow vindicated by extermination of Communists.[18]

Among the numerous pacifist organizations in the United
States, the Fellowship of Reconciliation (F.O.R.) is one of the
oldest and most prominent. Founded in 1915, F.O.R. has its
headquarters in Nyack, New York. In addition to producing
publications promoting peace, F.O.R. engages in demonstrations against war. The march on Washington in October, 1965,
in which from fifteen to twenty-five thousand marchers partici-
pated, was sponsored by F.O.R. Participants marched around
the White House protesting United States engagement in the
Vietnam conflict.

There appears to be a resurgence of pacifism among clergy-
men, as was true before World War II. Thousands of them are
protesting the war in Vietnam. By sermons, books, articles, and
participation in protest demonstrations, they are expressing
their opposition to war. A popular news magazine had a picture of a clergyman carrying a poster with the question:
"Would Christ Carry a Draft Card?"[19]

Perhaps the most powerful critic of pacifism is Reinhold
Niebuhr, former professor of Christian ethics at Union Theological Seminary in New York City. For him, Christianity is
not simply a new law of love, but measures the total dimension
of human existence in terms of both love and the fact of sin.
Most modern forms of pacifism, Niebuhr thinks, are heretical
because they are based upon the Renaissance belief in the
goodness of man, reject the Christian view of original sin, hold
that perfect love guarantees victory over the world, and reduces the Christian faith to the "simple gospel of Jesus."[20]

According to Niebuhr, the ethic of Jesus is an absolute "impossible possibility." There can be only approximations of such
an ethic. Pacifists simply dilute this ethic to justify their position. Even the most loving relations are not free from the
element of conflict that sin introduces into it. Refusal to recognize that sin injects an element of conflict into the world
invariably means that a morally perverse preference is given

to tyranny over war. Moreover, justice is dependent upon a balance of power. For example, women did not gain equality with men until they received sufficient economic power to challenge male autocracy.[21]

2. The Just War

Derived from the Stoics by the church fathers, the just war theory has been the general position of the church down to the present day. Ambrose introduced the concept into Christian thought with certain modifications. Augustine developed and popularized it, while Vittoria, a medieval moralist, completed it for the Roman Church.

Principal elements of the Christian doctrine of just war are as follows: (a) it must be just in its *intent,* namely, the restoration of peace, justice, and order; (b) it must *vindicate and establish justice;* (c) there must be a *reasonable hope for victory;* (d) decision to engage in war must be made by and waged under the *proper authority,* that is, the ruler or rulers of the state; (e) the *conduct* of war is to be just, that is, there must be no excessive, unnecessary violence and killing of civilians; (f) there should be no engagement in war except as a *last resort,* that is, after all means have been exhausted to keep the peace; (g) destruction imposed upon the enemy is to be measured by the principle of *proportionality,* namely, that the evil of the war be no greater than the evil to be corrected and a proper proportion between the degree of guilt and the scope of punishment; and (h) war must be waged in the spirit of love. This last principle is interpreted as an "inner disposition." That is, one is not to hate one's enemy, but to love him inwardly, though in combat it may mean taking his life. In other words, while one may not act agapeistically, one must have an agapeistic mind.

Some contemporary theologians believe that a just war is possible in a nuclear age. For example, Professor Paul Ramsey, of Princeton University, attempts, with certain modifications, to make the traditional view of the just war relevant for this nuclear age.[22] Between unlimited nuclear warfare and the complete rejection of force, Ramsey struggles to find the best possible answer that reason and religion have to offer.

Ramsey begins by noting that the early Christians were universally pacifists. But he argues that the changeover to the just war doctrine and practice was not a "fall" from the original purity of Christian ethics. Rather, it was a change in tactics.[23] He claims that early Christian advocates of the just war did not see it as a rejection of the commandment of love but as a fulfillment in service to men and the maintaining of the political and social order in which men live. This he calls love-informed justice.

Hence, the just war doctrine justified a defense of the moral order and at the same time limited the kind of war that could be justifiably fought. It is Ramsey's contention that the just war is applicable today and to depart from it is to surrender to irrationality and immorality.

But how *should* and how *shall* modern war be conducted justly? This is the central problem of Ramsey's work. The answer is by making a distinction between *counterforces* and *counterpeople* warfare. Thus, "noncombatant immunity" is the dominant theme of the just war tradition in his theory. From Augustine to the present, the basic rule of civilized warfare has meant the immunity of civilian populations from direct attack. Christian love demands this kind of responsible action. It also requires national or politically purposive armament and rational nuclear disarmament with prompt graduated unilateral steps in this direction by governments. This would leave only conventional weapons to be used in a just war.[24]

The basic principle of Ramsey's just war theory is that of *agapē*. Morally justified warfare is to be kept within the bounds of "faith active in love." The limitation placed upon conduct in the just war doctrine came, not from natural reason, but from humble moral reason under the Lordship of Christ, "as Christian men felt themselves impelled out of love to justify war and by love severely to limit war."[25]

Can the use of unlimited means of warfare ever be justified? Ramsey's conclusion is that the work of love will be to return ever again to the prohibition of direct killing of any person not directly or closely cooperating in the force that should be repelled. Thus, he makes much of the distinction between "direct" and "indirect" killing, between "intentional" and "unintentional" effects, a doctrine first formulated by Thomas Aquinas, the medieval theologian.[26]

In a more recent work, Ramsey presupposes as *regulative* the restrictions of the just war doctrine in the conduct of conventional and nuclear warfare. He defends the thesis that *counterforce* nuclear war is "the upper limit of rational, politically purposive military action."[27] Such restrictions would proscribe deliberate direct attack upon noncombatants and stress the primacy of counterforce warfare. On this basis, Ramsey discusses the "do-able" and the "un-do-able" in warfare.

Adopting a policy called "Counterforce plus Avoidance," Ramsey makes six proposals for policy decisions: (*a*) the United States and Western nations should "procure forces for sub-conventional and conventional warfare, and at the same time . . . repair in public consciousness a doctrine of the possible and just use of such forces"; (*b*) this nation should announce as a policy that we will never be the first to use nuclear weapons, "*except* tactical ones that may and will be used, against forces only and not strategically against an enemy's heartland, to stop an invasion across a clearly defined boundary, our own or one we are pledged by treaty to defend"; (*c*) strengthen conventional forces with the view to placing all nuclear arms in a class by themselves as weapons that may be possessed to deter the enemy from using his, but never to be used *first*, even in self-defense; (*d*) maintain nuclear weapons for use in counterforce strikes over enemy territory and to punish any violation of the rules that we have imposed upon ourselves prohibiting tactical, offensive use of such weapons over the territory of another nation; (*e*) a declaration by the United States that one of the consequences and purposes of limited war is *"to raise the risk of counterforce strategic war,"* not mutual destruction, with the aim of preserving a limit, not raising the risk; and (*f*) the preservation of power for "continual massive deterrence" with the *appearance of partial or possible* commitment to a policy we do not intend to carry out.[28]

Ramsey, a Methodist minister, may appear to be "out-Jesuiting Pascal's Jesuit."[29] But he does bring us face to face with the possibility of nuclear warfare and forces us to think about what is "do-able" and "un-do-able" in terms of his theory of the just war.

In the light of the destruction that would result from nuclear warfare, the just war doctrine raises a host of questions about its validity for today. It is repudiated as too simplistic and a rationalization to justify all wars. A summation of their arguments is in order. Exponents of the just war theory insist that a war must be *just in its intent*, namely, to restore peace and order. But can peace and order be restored after a multimegatonic catastrophe? Will not freedom be destroyed along with many of our cities and civilians? Would not a dictatorship be necessary to bring a semblance of order out of chaos? If we successfully destroy our military opponents along with hundreds of millions of civilians, how can we live with ourselves? What will happen to our spiritual, mental, and moral health? Will not those who suffer defeat hate us and as soon as possible seek revenge? May we not hear the cry of the prophet in a postnuclear holocaust: " 'Peace, peace,' when there is no peace"?

Another criterion of the just war is to *establish justice*. There must be a clear case of aggression with justice on one side only. But it is obviously difficult for a nation to be an objective judge of whether a war can be just only from its perspective. Inevitably there will be an element of subjectivity on both sides. Citizens of different nations and of the same religious faith have fought one another in recent major wars thinking that they were justified in doing so. Indeed, has there ever been an instance where people of a nation have refused to go to battle because they considered that their government was forcing them into an unjust war?

As to the matter that a just war may have a *reasonable hope for victory*, there is a question as to whether any nation will win in case of nuclear warfare. All the countries involved may compose the vanquished.

According to the just war doctrine, war must be waged under the *auspices of the ruler or the state*. But both ruler and government may be aggressive, corrupt, and predatory. Subjects could be fed false propaganda and a war could be made to appear to be justifiable. Indeed, the next great war may be fought by professionals and government leaders. If this is true, millions of people will experience obliteration without real representation.

There is a serious question as to whether a nuclear war can be just in *conduct*. Inevitably in any war a number of atrocities and a certain amount of wanton violence takes place. Noncombatants are hurt and many lose their lives. In a nuclear war, violence will be on a larger scale and millions of civilians will die.

The principle of the use of war as the *last resort* is problematic. How can a nation tell when all possible means for keeping the peace have been exhausted? May not the "war hawks" become impatient with prolonged negotiation, arbitration, and mediation efforts and lead their nation into war without patiently seeking a peaceful settlement?

The principle of *proportionality* is questionable as a guiding norm in nuclear warfare. Would not the evils that would follow a thermonuclear conflict be all out of proportion to the good obtained? Is there not the danger that a so-called "limited" war will escalate into a global war that may result in almost universal homicide? Who will be the judge as to how much devastation shall be wrought upon the enemy for injuries received? Infliction of punishment for small injuries is bound to be out of proportion to those received in a nuclear war.

Finally, is it really possible to keep a war under the control of *love*? How many soldiers can kill in battle with loving

hearts? Hatred of the enemy almost inevitably takes possession of those who witness the destruction caused by him.

3. The Holy Crusade

The holy crusade theory of war is based on the idea that a
war is holy because God wills it. To fight is a religious privilege, a service to God, and a way of salvation. For example,
the church of the Middle Ages engaged in eight crusades
against the Muslims in the Holy Land. The call to arms came
from the church and not from the political ruler. Even some
of the clergy and the monks joined the Crusades. Participation
in warfare was seen as a religious privilege against the enemies
of God.

Also the Reformed Churches tended toward the crusade in
their lack of tolerance toward dissenting religious groups, as
in Germany, where Lutheranism with the aid of the state per-
secuted the Anabaptists.[30] Likewise, Calvinism was imbued
with the crusade spirit in the subjection of Geneva to a theo-
cratic ideal and the protection of the same from attack by
Catholics.

In America, the Revolutionary War took on a crusading
quality, with the clergy giving vigorous support to the colonial
forces. Some of the churches of the Calvinistic tradition looked
upon the Civil War as a crusade against slavery. World War I
was regarded by most of the church groups as both a just and
holy crusade to eliminate war and to make the world safe for
democracy. World War II witnessed a decline of the crusading
spirit, and war came to be looked upon as "a grim business,"
a job that had to be done to preserve freedom. This is the pre-
vailing view toward the war in Vietnam which allegedly is
being prosecuted to contain communism and to honor our
commitment to a people whom we have promised to aid
against aggression.

War as a holy crusade declined in popularity after World
War I. Today only a few advocate such a position. Most of the
churches express a spirit of contrition about wars.

Generally, the holy crusade posture toward war is repugnant to modern man. It is not an easy thing for him to accept the notion that God wills war. He knows that Christians fighting one another claim that God is on their side.

D. TOWARD A VIABLE STANCE

Because of limitations of space, the above discussion touches only the broad outline of Christian attitudes toward participation in warfare. Inevitably one must come to some conclusions about the whole matter.

One is forced to appreciate the position of the redemptive pacifist based upon the example of Christ and the pattern of the early church. This type of pacifist should not be branded a coward. Indeed, he demonstrates personal courage. His radical nonresistance is due, not to fear of war, but faithfulness to his conviction that war is a violation of his Christian conscience.

On the other hand, the pacifist position betrays a weakness in that it stresses absolute love at the expense of justice in both personal and social relations. Because of the sinful nature of man and nations, some form of coercive action is necessary to maintain order and justice. Paul recognized this fact in his view of the state in Rom. 13:1-7. If a nation is to survive, it must protect its people from aggression. It can do this only through the support of its citizens. Moreover, there is no prohibition in the Scriptures against Christians serving in the government as judges, policemen, or even in the military. Governing authorities are God's servants, and as long as the state fulfills its purpose of punishing the evil and protecting the good, it does the will of God (Rom. 13:1-7). Soldiering appears to be morally acceptable in the New Testament, because there is no instance where soldiers are commanded to withdraw from such service. (See Luke 3:14; 7:1-10; John 4:46-53.)

The holy crusade in which the Christian soldier can fight with the assurance that he is wielding "the sword of the Lord and Gideon" is highly questionable. War is not holy. At the most, the *cause* of war—freedom, defense against the aggressor, justice—may be holy. Much at stake in a war may be holy, but never war itself.

This leaves us with the adoption of some modified form of the just war doctrine. Between the positions of the absolute pacifist, who refuses to serve in governmental roles, and that of the holy war advocate, who identifies war with the will of God, is there a more realistic one? The following statements do not propose to be the *via media,* but to suggest possible steps in that direction.

War may be justifiable for self-defense to protect a nation's rights against an aggressor. A nation could hardly survive without the right to defend itself. However, aggressive warfare is unjustifiable. One must decide for himself as to the justifiability of certain wars. This means that the individual has the right to choose which war he will support. During World War II, for example, John Bennett, now president of Union Theological Seminary in New York City, supported, along with his fellow "Christian realists," the war against Hitler. Today, he rejects the arguments given by our government to aid military actions in Vietnam.[31]

To follow one's conscience in choosing a particular conflict in which to participate requires a hard look at all the issues involved. Alan Geyer,[32] director for international relations, Council for Christian Social Action, United Church of Christ, thinks that the classic just war doctrine supports principles by which the Selective Service law might be revised so as to allow for anyone whose objection is limited to participating in a particular war. He suggests criteria that may define a "selective objector" posture. They are as follows: (1) present evidence of serious examination of the issues of a particular war in which he feels he cannot participate; (2) provide evidence that "he is capable of serious effort at moral reasoning in the attempt to relate his convictions to the data he possesses"; (3) demonstrate that he has attempted to give "political expression" to his convictions; (4) make it known that he is willing to participate in a military role other than the war to which he objects; and (5) accept whatever legal penalties his stand may impose upon him.[33]

Geyer's view may provide a viable posture toward war for the Christian who cannot accept either the pacifist or the holy crusade theories. However, the decision should be informed by Biblical realism, the just war theory, and the issues at stake in a particular war.

Certainly Christians must never uncritically accept every national policy or place national interests above commitment to Christ. When the demands of Caesar clash with the claims of Christ, Christians must take their stand with Peter and John, who declared, "We must obey God rather than men" (Acts 5:29).

Ultimately, the Christian himself will have to decide about participation in actual warfare. Should he engage in battle, he will do so with heaviness of heart for all the suffering it will inflict upon others. No doubt he will be plagued with an uneasy conscience and haunted by the example of Jesus, the stance of the early church, and the fact that in wars Christians kill Christians. If a Christian chooses not to support a war or to fight, he must courageously face criticism and possible imprisonment.

Meanwhile, the church has a role to play in maintaining the peace. When Japan signed the surrender treaty in 1945, General MacArthur declared: "The problem [of war] basically is theological, and involves a spiritual recrudescence and improvement of human character. It must be of the spirit if we are to save the flesh." The task of the church is primarily in the realm of the spirit and the character of men. Its task is the proclamation and demonstration of the gospel of repentance, reconciliation, and peacemaking.

Some of the practical things the church can do are to think and will peace; urge the continuation of negotiations and multilateral disarmament of nuclear weapons (unilateral disarmament would be an invitation to a Communist take-over. Nuclear parity appears to be a factor in keeping the peace. While this agonizing "balance of terror" is not an ideal solution to the problem of war, so far it has restrained both the United States and the U.S.S.R. from attacking each other); build bridges of understanding between people of all nations; keep alive the Biblical ideal of peace (Isa. 2:1 ff.); pray for peace; and explore the possibility of establishing some form of world government in which national egoism may be subordinated to the common good of mankind.

NOTES

CHAPTER I   The New Theology: "God Is Dead"

1. See also "The Empty Cradle," *Theology Today*, Jan., 1957; "The Great Whatever," *The Nation*, March 7, 1959; "This Post-Christian Era," *The Nation*, Dec. 12, 1959; "The God We Deserve," *The Nation*, Feb. 20, 1960; "Plea for a New Reformation," *The Nation*, April 16, 1960; "The Lost Iconoclasm of Christianity," *The Nation*, April 22, 1961; "Beyond the Death of God: The Need of Cultural Revolution," *Dialog*, Autumn, 1962; and "Swallowed Up by Godlessness," *The Christian Century*, Dec. 8, 1965.

2. Gabriel Vahanian, *The Death of God* (George Braziller, Inc., 1961), pp. 49–51.

3. *Ibid.*, pp. 199, 201.

4. *Ibid.*, pp. 75–78.

5. Paul van Buren, "Theology in the Context of Culture," *The Christian Century*, April 17, 1965, pp. 428–430.

6. See especially "A Secular Theology for a World Come of Age," *Theology Today*, Jan., 1962, pp. 435–459; "Thursday's Child: The Theologian Today and Tomorrow," *Theology Today*, Jan., 1964, pp. 487–495; and "The Shape of a Radical Theology," *The Christian Century*, Oct. 6, 1965, pp. 1219–1222.

7. William Hamilton, *The New Essence of Christianity* (Association Press, 1961), Ch. 1, "On Theological Style."

8. *Ibid.*, p. 65.

9. *Ibid.*, p. 59.

10. See especially "Nirvana and the Kingdom of God," *Journal of Religion*, April, 1963; "Creative Negation in Theology," *The Christian Century*, July 7, 1965, pp. 864–867; and "Word and History," *Theology Today*, Oct., 1965, pp. 380–393.

11. Altizer, "Creative Negation in Theology," *loc. cit.*, p. 864.

12. Altizer, "Word and History," *loc. cit.*, p. 380.

13. Friedrich Nietzsche, *Thus Spake Zarathustra*, Part III, Ch. 52, par. 2, in *The Philosophy of Nietzsche* (George Allen & Unwin, Ltd.; The Modern Library, Inc., 1927), p. 202. Quotations used by permission of the publishers, George Allen & Unwin, Ltd.

14. *Ibid.*, Part IV, Ch. 67, p. 297.

15. Paul van Buren, *The Secular Meaning of the Gospel* (The Macmillan Company, 1963), p. 1; Dietrich Bonhoeffer, *Prisoner for God*, ed. by Eberhard Bethge, tr. by Reginald H. Fuller (The Macmillan Company, 1953), p. 163. *The Secular Meaning of the Gospel*, copyright © 1963 by The Macmillan Company. Quotations used by permission of the publishers.

16. Hamilton, "The Shape of a Radical Theology," *loc. cit.*, p. 1220. Copyright 1965, Christian Century Foundation. Quotations used by permission of *The Christian Century*.

17. Van Buren, *The Secular Meaning of the Gospel*, p. 104.

18. Thomas J. J. Altizer and William Hamilton, *Radical Theology and the Death of God* (The Bobbs-Merrill Company, Inc., 1966), p. 126.

19. Altizer, "Creative Negation in Theology," *loc. cit.*, p. 866.

20. Vahanian, *The Death of God*, p. xxxii.

21. *Ibid.*, Ch. 8.

22. Altizer and Hamilton, *op. cit.*, p. 33.

23. *Ibid.*, p. xii.

24. *Ibid.*, p. 47.

25. Thomas J. J. Altizer, *The Gospel of Christian Atheism* (The Westminster Press, 1966), p. 67.

26. Hamilton, "The Shape of a Radical Theology," *loc. cit.*, p. 1221.

27. Vahanian, *The Death of God*, p. 20.

28. *Ibid.*, p. 25.

29. *Ibid.*, p. 231.

30. Van Buren, *The Secular Meaning of the Gospel*, p. 54.

31. *Ibid.*, p. 125.

32. Altizer, "Creative Negation in Theology," *loc. cit.*, p. 866. Copyright 1965, Christian Century Foundation. Quotations used by permission of *The Christian Century*.

33. Altizer, *The Gospel of Christian Atheism*, p. 61.

34. *Ibid.*, p. 68.

35. *Ibid.*, p. 71.

36. *Ibid.*, p. 73.

37. *Ibid.*, pp. 74–75.

38. Altizer, "Creative Negation in Theology," *loc. cit.*, p. 866.

39. Altizer, "Word and History," *loc. cit.*, p. 393.

40. See van Buren, *The Secular Meaning of the Gospel*, Ch. I.

41. Hamilton, "The Shape of a Radical Theology," *loc. cit.*, p. 1221.

42. "The 'God Is Dead' Movement," *Time*, Oct. 22, 1965, p. 62.

43. Julian Huxley, *Religion Without Revelation*, rev. ed. (Harper & Brothers, 1957), p. 58.

44. William Hamilton, *The Christian Man* (The Westminster Press, 1956), Ch. 2.

45. Hamilton, *The New Essence of Christianity*, Ch. 4.

46. "The 'God Is Dead' Movement," *loc. cit.*, p. 62; Altizer and Hamilton, *op. cit.*, p. 92.

47. *Ibid.*

48. Hamilton, "Thursday's Child," *loc. cit.*, p. 495.

49. Thomas J. J. Altizer, *Oriental Mysticism and Biblical Eschatology* (The Westminster Press, 1961), pp. 93–101, 179–189.

50. *Ibid.*, p. 95.

51. Van Buren, *The Secular Meaning of the Gospel*, p. 125.

52. *Ibid.*, pp. 125–126.

53. *Ibid.*, p. 132; Bonhoeffer, *Prisoner for God*, p. 179.

54. See Paul L. Holmer, "Contra the New Theologies," *The Christian Century*, March 17, 1965, pp. 329–332; and a group of articles on "Death-of-God: Four Views," *The Christian Century*, Nov. 17, 1965.

55. Hamilton, *The New Essence of Christianity*, p. 65; Altizer and Hamilton, *op. cit.*, p. 28.

56. J. Robert Nelson, "Deicide, Theothanasia, or What Do You Mean?" *The Christian Century*, Nov. 17, 1965, p. 1415.

57. *Ibid.*, p. 1416.

58. Daniel Day Williams, in *Time*, Oct. 22, 1965, p. 62.

59. Langdon Gilkey, "Dissolution and Reconstruction in Theology," *The Christian Century*, Feb. 3, 1965, p. 138. Copyright 1965, Christian Century Foundation. Quotation used by permission of *The Christian Century*.

60. Hamilton, "Thursday's Child," *loc. cit.*, pp. 489–490.

61. Altizer and Hamilton, *op. cit.*, p. 15; Altizer, *The Gospel of Christian Atheism*, pp. 9–10.

62. Hamilton, "Thursday's Child," *loc. cit.*, p. 493. Quotations used by permission of *Theology Today*.

63. *Ibid.*, p. 495.

64. Van Buren, *The Secular Meaning of the Gospel*, p. 191.

65. Van Buren, "Theology in the Context of Culture," *loc. cit.*, p. 430.

66. John Bennett, "In Defense of God," *Look*, April 19, 1966, pp. 69–70; 72, 75, 76.

67. Billy Graham, *U.S. News & World Report*, April 25, 1966, pp. 74–82.

68. John Baillie, *The Sense of the Presence of God* (Charles Scribner's Sons, 1962), p. 53.

69. Philip Schaff and Henry Wace, eds., *Nicene and Post-Nicene*

Fathers (Wm. B. Eerdmans Publishing Company, 1956), "The Confessions of St. Augustine," Vol. I, p. 45.

70. John R. Claypool, "The Death of God," *Crescent Hill Sermons,* Vol. I, No. 27 (Nov. 7, 1965).

CHAPTER II   The New Ethics: "Love Alone"

1. Sidney Cave, *The Christian Way* (Philosophical Library, Inc., 1951) p. 5.

2. Robert Moskin, "Morality USA," *Look,* Sept. 24, 1963, p. 74.

3. Harlow Shapley, "Stars, Ethics, and Survival," *Religion in Life,* Vol. XXX (Summer, 1961), p. 341.

4. Thomas C. Oden, *Radical Obedience: The Ethics of Rudolf Bultmann* (The Westminster Press, 1964), p. 25; Rudolf Bultmann, *Jesus and the Word* (Charles Scribner's Sons, 1958), pp. 75 ff.; and Rudolf Bultmann, *Jesus Christ and Mythology* (Charles Scribner's Sons, 1958), pp. 11–21.

5. Rudolf Bultmann, *Theology of the New Testament,* tr. by Kendrick Grobel (Charles Scribner's Sons, 1951), Vol. I, pp. 19–21.

6. Bultmann, *Jesus and the Word,* pp. 71–72.

7. Bultmann, *Theology of the New Testament,* Vol. I, pp. 18–19.

8. Bultmann, *Jesus and the Word,* p. 115.

9. Oden, *op. cit.,* pp. 48–56.

10. Bultmann, *Essays: Philosophical and Theological* (London: SCM Press, 1955), pp. 95 ff.

11. John A. T. Robinson, *Honest to God* (London: SCM Press and The Westminster Press, 1963).

12. David L. Edwards, ed., *The Honest to God Debate* (London: SCM Press and The Westminster Press, 1963).

13. Robinson, *Honest to God,* p. 76.

14. *Ibid.,* p. 82.

15. Joseph Fletcher, *Situation Ethics: The New Morality* (The Westminster Press, 1966), p. 34.

16. John A. T. Robinson, *Christian Morals Today* (The Westminster Press, 1964), pp. 12–13.

17. *Ibid.,* p. 46.

18. *Ibid.,* p. 16.

19. *Ibid.,* pp. 36–37.

20. *Ibid.,* pp. 25–26.

21. *Ibid.,* p. 40.

22. Robinson, *Honest to God,* p. 115.

23. *Ibid.*

24. *Ibid.,* p. 117.

25. Fletcher, *Situation Ethics,* pp. 17–39.

26. *Ibid.,* p. 31.

27. *Ibid.,* p. 33.

28. *Ibid.,* p. 52.

29. *Ibid.,* p. 54.

30. *Ibid.,* pp. 69–144; also in brief form in "Six Propositions: The New Look in Christian Ethics," *Harvard Divinity Bulletin,* October, 1959, pp. 7–18.

31. Fletcher, "Six Propositions: The New Look in Christian Ethics," *loc. cit.,* p. 10. Quotations used by permission of *Harvard Divinity Bulletin.*

32. *Ibid.*

33. *Ibid.,* pp. 11–12; also Fletcher, *Situation Ethics,* pp. 91, 95.

34. Fletcher, "Six Propositions: The New Look in Christian Ethics," *loc. cit.,* p. 14.

35. *Ibid.*

36. *Ibid.*

37. *Ibid.,* p. 15; see Emil Brunner, *The Divine Imperative* (The Westminster Press, 1947), p. 132.

38. Fletcher, "Six Propositions: The New Look in Christian Ethics," *loc. cit.,* p. 16.

39. *Ibid.,* p. 17.

40. Fletcher, *Situation Ethics,* p. 148.

41. *Ibid.,* p. 158.

42. Fletcher, "Six Propositions: The New Look in Christian Ethics," *loc. cit.,* p. 18.

43. Fletcher, *Situation Ethics,* p. 158.

44. Seward Hiltner's review of Fletcher's *Situation Ethics* in *Pastoral Psychology,* May, 1966, p. 55.

45. James Gustafson, "How Does Love Reign?" *The Christian Century,* May 18, 1966, p. 654.

46. Rule-agapism seeks to determine which rules of action are most love-embodying, and act-agapism, which acts are most loving—terms in the ethical typology of William Frankena, *Ethics* (Prentice-Hall, Inc., 1963), pp. 42–44. For examples of Robinson's vacillations between these two positions, see Paul Ramsey, *Deeds and Rules in Christian Ethics* (London and Edinburgh: Oliver & Boyd, Ltd., 1965), pp. 15–27.

47. Robinson, *Honest to God,* pp. 116–117; Fletcher, *Situation Ethics,* pp. 85–86.

48. James Gustafson, in Martin E. Marty and Dean G. Peerman, eds., *New Theology, No. 3* (The Macmillan Company, 1966), "Context Versus Principles: A Misplaced Debate in Christian Ethics," p. 70.

49. *Ibid.,* pp. 69–99.

50. J. H. Spencer, *History of Kentucky Baptists from 1769–1885* (J. R. Baumes, 1885), Vol. I, pp. 355–356.

51. Fletcher, *Situation Ethics,* pp. 95–96.

52. Robinson, *Christian Morals Today,* p. 16.

53. Ramsey, *op. cit.,* pp. 94–99.

54. *Ibid.,* pp. 100–110.

55. Bultmann, *Jesus and the Word,* p. 88.

56. Robinson, *Christian Morals Today,* p. 32.

57. See John C. Bennett, "Ethical Principles and the Context," *Year Book 1960–1961,* The American Society of Christian Ethics, Report of the Second Annual Meeting, Evanston, Illinois, ed. by Das Kelley Barnett, 1961, pp. 9–19.

58. See Henlee H. Barnette, *Introducing Christian Ethics* (Broadman Press, 1961), Ch. X, "Ethics of the Holy Spirit."

CHAPTER III   The New Sex Code: "Permissiveness with Affection"

1. Reinhold Niebuhr, "Sex Standards in America," *Christianity and Crisis,* Vol. VIII, No. 9 (May 24, 1948), p. 65.

2. Ernest Hemingway, in "The Second Sexual Revolution," *Time,* Jan. 24, 1964, p. 54.

3. Ira L. Reiss, "The Double Standard in Premarital Sexual Intercourse; A Neglected Concept," *Social Forces,* Vol. XXXIV, No. 3 (March, 1956), pp. 224–230.

4. See Roland H. Bainton, in Simon Doniger, ed., *Sex and Religion Today* (Association Press, 1953), pp. 17–89.

5. See Kimball Young, *Sociology* (American Book Company, 1949), pp. 325–326; and Pearl S. Buck, "The Sexual Revolution," *Ladies' Home Journal,* Sept., 1964, pp. 43 ff.

6. Roger Shinn, *Tangled World* (Charles Scribner's Sons, 1965), p. 131.

7. Ira L. Reiss, in "The Second Sexual Revolution," *loc. cit.,* p. 56.

8. *Ibid.,* p. 57.

9. Benjamin DeMott, "The Anatomy of 'Playboy,'" *Commentary,* Vol. 34 (August, 1962), pp. 111–119.

10. Introductory statement to the article by Darrell L. Guder, "Who Is Man and What Is Love?" *Eternity,* Vol. 15 (Oct., 1964), p. 23. Used by permission of *Eternity* magazine.

11. *Playboy,* Feb., 1964, p. 144.

12. *Ibid.*

13. *Ibid.*

14. Hugh Hefner, "The Playboy Forum," *Playboy,* Feb., 1964, p. 149. Quotations from *Playboy* used by permission of the publishers.

15. *Playboy*, Feb., 1964, p. 47.

16. *Ibid.*, p. 143.

17. *Playboy*, April, 1964, p. 177.

18. "An Empire Built on Sex," *Life*, Oct. 29, 1965, pp. 68A–69B.

19. "Playboy Sermon," *Playboy*, March, 1965, pp. 47–48, 138–139.

20. Hugh Hefner, "The Playboy Philosophy," *Playboy*, July, 1963, pp. 49–50.

21. *Ibid.*, Dec., 1963, p. 70.

22. *Ibid.*, Dec., 1962, p. 4.

23. *Ibid.*, p. 5.

24. "An Empire Built on Sex," *Life*, Oct. 29, 1965, p. 71. Quotation used by permission of the publishers.

25. Shinn, *op. cit.*, p. 135.

26. *Ibid.*, p. 131.

27. *Ibid.*

28. "The Second Sexual Revolution," *loc. cit.*, p. 57.

29. *Ibid.*

30. Robinson, *Honest to God*, p. 119.

31. *Ibid.*

32. Robinson, *Christian Morals Today*, p. 45.

33. From *No New Morality*, pp. 86–87. Copyright © 1964 by Douglas Rhymes; reprinted by permission of the publishers, The Bobbs-Merrill Company, Inc.

34. *Ibid.*, p. 87.

35. H. A. Williams in Alexander R. Vidler, ed., *Soundings* (Cambridge: Cambridge University Press, 1962), pp. 81–82. Quotation used by permission of the publishers.

36. "Morality," *Time*, March 5, 1965, p. 44. Quotations used by permission of *Time*, Inc.

37. *Ibid.*

38. *Ibid.*

39. Robinson, *Honest to God*, p. 117.

40. Editorial, *Christianity Today*, March 12, 1965, pp. 29–30.

41. "Morality," *loc. cit.*, p. 44.

42. Paul Ramsey, "A Christian Approach to the Question of Sexual Relations Outside of Marriage," reprint from *The Journal of Religion*, Vol. XLV, No. 2 (April, 1965).

43. *Ibid.*, p. 108.

44. *Ibid.*, p. 113.

45. Richard A. McCormick, "Toward a New Sexual Morality?" *The Catholic World*, Oct. 25, 1965, pp. 10–16.

46. *Ibid.*, p. 12.

47. *Ibid.*, p. 16.

48. *Ibid.*

49. Robert E. Fitch, "A Common Sense Sex Code," *The Christian Century,* Oct. 7, 1964, pp. 1233–1235.

50. *Ibid.,* p. 1233. Copyright 1964, Christian Century Foundation. Quotations used by permission of *The Christian Century.*

51. *Ibid.,* pp. 1234–1235.

52. Seward Hiltner, *Sex Ethics and the Kinsey Reports* (Association Press, 1953).

53. *Ibid.,* p. 40.

54. Derrick Sherwin Bailey, *The Mystery of Love and Marriage* (Harper & Brothers, 1952), p. 46. Quotations used by permission of the publishers.

55. *Ibid.*

56. Otto Piper, *The Christian Interpretation of Sex* (Charles Scribner's Sons, 1951), pp. 52–57.

57. Bailey, *op. cit.,* pp. 51–52.

58. See Helmut Thielicke, *The Ethics of Sex,* tr. by John W. Doberstein (Harper & Row, Publishers, Inc., 1964), p. 94.

59. William G. Cole, *Sex and Love in the Bible* (Association Press, 1959), pp. 253–254. Quoted by permission of the publishers.

60. Thielicke, *op. cit.,* pp. 90–94.

61. *Ibid.,* p. 93.

62. Emil Brunner, *The Divine Imperative,* p. 347.

63. *Ibid.*

64. Evelyn Duvall, *Why Wait Till Marriage?* (Association Press, 1965).

65. Evelyn Duvall and Reuben Hill, *Being Married* (D. C. Heath and Company, 1960), pp. 408–410.

66. Grace and Fred M. Hechinger, *Teen-Age Tyranny* (William Morrow and Company, Inc., 1963), Chs. 6–10.

CHAPTER IV The New Church: "Servant in a Secular Society"

1. See *The Encyclopaedia Britannica,* Vol. XXIV (Cambridge, England: University Press, 11th ed., 1911), pp. 572–573.

2. John C. Bennett, *Christianity and Our World* (Association Press, 1943), p. 1.

3. Langdon Gilkey, *How the Church Can Minister to the World Without Losing Itself* (Harper & Row, Publishers, Inc., 1964), pp. 20–21. Quotations used by permission of the publishers.

4. John Richard Spann, ed., *The Christian Faith and Secularism* (Abingdon-Cokesbury Press, 1948), p. 11.

5. Cox, *op. cit.,* p. 21.

6. Georgia Harkness, *The Modern Rival of the Christian Faith* (Abingdon Press, 1952), p. 16.

7. Charles West, "Community—Christian and Secular," *Man in Community*, ed. by Egbert de Vries (Association Press, 1966), p. 343. Quotations used by permission of the World Council of Churches.

8. D. L. Munby, *The Idea of a Secular Society* (London: Oxford University Press, 1963), pp. 14–35.

9. Harvey Cox, *The Secular City* (The Macmillan Company, 1965), "Introduction," pp. 1–13.

10. *Ibid.*, Ch. 2.

11. *Ibid.*, p. 60.

12. *Ibid.*, pp. 83–84.

13. *Ibid.*, Ch. 1; West, in de Vries, ed., *op. cit.*, pp. 348–351; Friedrich Gogarten, *Verhängnis und Hoffnung der Neuzeit* (Stuttgart: Friedrich Vorwerk Verlag, 1953) and *Der Mensch zwischen Gott und Welt* (Stuttgart: Friedrich Vorwerk Verlag, 1956).

14. Cox, *op. cit.*, p. 21.

15. *Ibid.*, pp. 25–26.

16. See John T. McNeill, *The Christian Faith and Secularism*, "Historical Introduction to Secularism," pp. 24–42.

17. "Secularism," *The Encyclopedia Americana* (1958), Vol. 24, p. 521.

18. Steven Mackie, "European Christians and the Secular Debate," *Student World* (Geneva: World Student Christian Federation), Vol. 56, No. 1 (1963), pp. 4–12; Martin Jarrett-Kerr, *The Secular Promise* (Fortress Press, 1964), Ch. 1.

19. Norman Vincent Peale, *The Power of Positive Thinking* (Prentice-Hall, Inc., 1953), pp. 55 f., 63–64.

20. William H. Whyte, Jr., *The Organization Man* (Doubleday & Company, Inc., 1957), p. 407.

21. J. Milton Yinger, *Religion, Society and the Individual* (The Macmillan Company, 1957), Part I, pp. 25–26; American Institute of Public Opinion, "Public Opinion Service," March 20, 1955.

22. T. S. Eliot, *The Idea of a Christian Society* (Harcourt, Brace and World, Inc., 1940), pp. 86–87.

23. Karl Heim, *Christian Faith and Natural Science* (Harper & Brothers, 1957), p. 24. Quoted by permission of the publishers.

24. Cited by Gabriel Vahanian, *The Death of God*, p. 150.

25. To cite a few: John A. T. Robinson, *Honest to God*, Ch. 4; Cox, *op. cit.*, Chs. 5, 11; C. B. Armstrong, in Martin E. Marty and Dean G. Peerman, eds., *New Theology No. 2* (The Macmillan Company, 1965), "Christianity Without Religion," pp. 17–27; William O. Fennell, in Marty and Peerman, eds., *New Theology No. 2*, "The Theology of True

Secularity," pp. 28–38; Daniel Callahan, in Marty and Peerman, eds., *New Theology No. 3*, "The Secular City: Toward a Theology of Secularity," pp. 30–39.

26. Wilhelm Dantine, "The Revelation of Man," *Student World*, Vol. 56, No. 1 (1963), p. 30.

27. André Dumas, "Contagious Humanity," *Student World*, Vol. 56, No. 1 (1963), p. 61.

28. Dietrich Bonhoeffer, *Ethics*, ed. by Eberhard Bethge and tr. by Neville Horton Smith (London: SCM Press, Ltd., 1955; The Macmillan Company, 1955), p. 64. Copyright © 1955, The Macmillan Company. Quotations used by permission of the publishers.

29. *Ibid.*, pp. 84–100.

30. J. C. Hoekendijk, *The Church Inside Out*, tr. by Isaac C. Rottenberg (The Westminster Press, 1964), p. 71.

31. *Ibid.*, p. 72.

32. John A. T. Robinson, *The New Reformation?* (The Westminster Press, 1965), p. 42.

33. M. Richard Shaull, in Marty and Peerman, eds., *New Theology No. 2*, "The Form of the Church in the Modern Diaspora," p. 287.

34. Hoekendijk, *op. cit.*, p. 79.

35. Dietrich Bonhoeffer, *Christ the Center*, tr. by John Bowden (Harper & Row, Publishers, Inc., 1966), pp. 59–60.

36. See Hoekendijk, *op. cit.*, Ch. V; Shaull, in Marty and Peerman, eds., *New Theology No. 2*, pp. 275–287; Stephen Rose, ed., *Who's Killing the Church?* (Chicago City Missionary Society, 1966).

37. Gibson Winter, *The New Creation as Metropolis* (The Macmillan Company, 1963), p. 10.

38. Gibson Winter, *The Suburban Captivity of the Churches* (Doubleday & Company, Inc., 1961), p. 170.

39. Paul L. Lehmann, *Ethics in a Christian Context* (Harper & Row, Publishers, Inc., 1963), pp. 81–95.

40. Cox, *op. cit.*, p. 255.

41. *Ibid.*, Ch. 6, p. 256.

42. Archie Hargraves, "Go Where the Action Is," *Social Action*, Feb., 1964, p. 17; cited by Cox, *op. cit.*, pp. 125–126.

43. George W. Webber, *The Congregation in Mission* (Abingdon Press, 1964), p. 170. Quotations used by permission of the publishers.

44. *Ibid.*, p. 171.

45. Philippe Maury, *Politics and Evangelism* (Doubleday & Company, Inc., 1959), Ch. V.

46. See Robinson, *The New Reformation?* pp. 35 f., 47, 50.

47. Webber, *op. cit.*, p. 62.

48. Winter, *The New Creation as Metropolis*, pp. 92 ff.

49. Robinson, *Honest to God,* pp. 87–88.

50. *Ibid.,* pp. 92–93, 97, 99.

51. *Ibid.,* pp. 92, 104.

52. Gilkey, *How the Church Can Minister to the World Without Losing Itself,* pp. 22–23.

53. *Ibid.,* p. 23.

54. D. L. Munby, *op. cit.,* p. 77.

55. Gilkey, *How the Church Can Minister to the World Without Losing Itself,* p. 23.

56. Edwin E. Aubrey, *Secularism a Myth* (Harper & Brothers, 1954), pp. 105, 134.

57. See E. L. Mascall, *The Secularization of Christianity* (Holt, Rinehart and Winston, Inc., 1965).

58. Bonhoeffer, *Ethics,* pp. 79 ff.

59. Gayraud S. Wilmore, *The Secular Relevance of the Church* (The Westminster Press, 1962), p. 25.

60. *Ibid.,* pp. 31–36.

61. John A. T. Robinson, *Sunday Mirror,* Dec. 22, 1963, cited by Mascall, *op. cit.,* p. 147.

62. *Ibid.,* p. 147; see also Edwards, ed., *op. cit.,* pp. 265–267, where Robinson has a more cautious statement about his views on the virgin birth and the resurrection of Jesus.

63. Robinson, *Honest to God,* Ch. 4.

64. Bonhoeffer, *Ethics,* p. 89.

65. See Henlee H. Barnette, *Christian Calling and Vocation* (Baker Book House, 1965).

66. James H. Nichols, *Primer for Protestants* (Association Press, 1947), p. 138.

CHAPTER V *The New Dimensions of War:*
  "Thinking About the Unthinkable"

1. Arnold J. Toynbee, *War and Civilization* (Oxford University Press, 1950), p. 12.

2. Brunner, *op. cit.,* p. 469.

3. Henry P. Fairchild, ed., *Dictionary of Sociology* (Philosophical Library, 1944), p. 336.

4. See Pitirim Sorokin, *Society, Culture, and Personality* (Harper & Brothers, 1947), pp. 496–497.

5. G. Curtis Jones, "Pulpit Paragraphs," *The Pulpit,* Vol. XXV, No. 5 (May, 1954), p. 28.

6. "The War in Viet Nam," *Newsweek,* March 14, 1966, p. 41.

7. The title that Herman Kahn has given one of his books: *Thinking*

About the Unthinkable (Horizon Press, 1962).

8. David R. Inglis, "The Nature of Nuclear War," *Nuclear Weapons and the Conflict of Conscience,* John C. Bennett, ed. (Charles Scribner's Sons, 1962), p. 43.

9. Harrison Brown and James Real, *Community of Fear* (Center for the Study of Democratic Institutions, 1960), pp. 13–20.

10. *Ibid.,* p. 18.

11. Roland H. Bainton, *Christian Attitudes Toward War and Peace* (Abingdon Press, 1960).

12. C. J. Cadoux, *The Early Church and the World* (Edinburgh: T. & T. Clark, 1955), pp. 269–286; 402–442; 564–596.

13. See Charles Raven, *The Theological Basis of Christian Pacificism* (Fellowship Publications, 1951); and Culbert Rutenber, *The Dagger and the Cross* (Fellowship Publications, 1950).

14. Bainton, *Christian Attitudes Toward War and Peace,* p. 253.

15. *Ibid.,* p. 265.

16. *Ibid.,* p. 267.

17. *A Christian Approach to Nuclear War* (Church Peace Mission, New York City, n.d.), p. 10.

18. *Ibid.,* pp. 11–12.

19. *Newsweek,* November 15, 1965, p. 78.

20. Reinhold Niebuhr, *Christianity and Power Politics* (Charles Scribner's Sons, 1952), pp. 5–6.

21. *Ibid.,* pp. 25–26.

22. See Paul Ramsey, *War and the Christian Conscience* (Duke University Press, 1961).

23. *Ibid.,* p. xvii.

24. *Ibid.,* p. 308.

25. *Ibid.,* p. 59.

26. *Ibid.,* pp. xix–xx; 34–59.

27. Paul Ramsey, *The Limits of Nuclear War: Thinking About the Do-Able and the Un-Do-Able* (The Council on Religion and International Affairs, 1963), p. 10. Quotations used by permission of the Council.

28. *Ibid.,* pp. 30–41.

29. James H. Smylie, in his review of Ramsey's *The Limits of Nuclear War* in *The Christian Century,* Oct. 23, 1963, p. 1309.

30. Roland H. Bainton, "The Churches and War: Historic Attitudes Toward Christian Participation," *Social Action,* Jan. 15, 1945, p. 22.

31. John Bennett, "Christian Realism in Vietnam," *America,* April 30, 1966, p. 616.

32. Alan Geyer, "The Just War and the Selective Objector," *The Christian Century,* Feb. 16, 1966, pp. 199–201.

33. *Ibid.,* p. 201.